VISUAL DESIGN | ON THE

D1415432

VISUAL DESIGN | ON THE COMPUTER

wucius wong / benjamin wong

Design Books

Printed in the United States of America

Designed by Benjamin Wong

Copyright © 1994 by Wucius Wong and Benjamin Wong

Reproduction or republication of the content in any manner, without the express written permission of the publisher, is prohibited. The publisher takes no responsibility for the use of any of the materials or methods described in this book, or for the products thereof.

Library of Congress Cataloging-in-Publication Data

Wong, Wucius.
   Visual design on the computer / Wucius Wong and Benjamin Wong.
         p. cm.
   Includes bibliographical reference and index.
   ISBN 1-55821-298-1
   1. Computer-aided design. I. Wong, Benjamin. I. Title
  TA174.W588 1994   94-1100
  745.4--dc20   CIP

Published by Design Books

Design Books are distributed by
Lyons & Burford, Publishers
31 West 21st Street
New York NY 10010

5 4 3 2

Disclaimer
Trademarked names appear throughout this book. Rather than list the names and entities that own the trademarks or insert a trademark symbol with each mention of the trademarked name, the publisher states that it is using the names only for editorial purposes and to the benefit of the trademark owner, with no intention of infringing upon that trademark.

TO PANSY

Designing on the computer has become a relatively simple operation. With proper software, all of us can make lines and shapes and master the basics in a few hours.

With the computer, professional designers can probe into wider options and visualize ideas with greater efficiency, and nondesigners may improve the appearance of anything they produce for printing. We have entered a time in which whoever designs must know how to use the computer, and whoever uses the computer for the presentation of any information may have to do some design work.

Computer training is already an integral part of design training. Designers who are used only to traditional tools may have to become computer literate to adapt themselves to the new situation.

This book has been written to meet such needs. It actually offers a structured course enabling anyone to learn design fundamentals and computer techniques. It further aims to provide practicing designers with a new vocabulary and grammar—a new visual language that blends with computer language.

Fifteen learning sessions are contained in fifteen chapters, covering essentially the visual aspects of design—which we refer to as visual design—and including ways and means to attain desired results on the computer. Each section contains numerous valuable ideas, methods, and tips that can be put into ready use. Nearly a thousand diagrams and illustrations accompany the text.

Chapter 1 defines visual design and offers advice on course planning and evaluation of results. Chapter 2 introduces computer equipment, with recommendations on essential graphics programs. Chapters 3 to 6 cover basic techniques with draw programs. Chapters 7 and 8 discuss paint and image-editing programs. Chapters 9 to 14 concentrate on design concepts. Chapter 15 tackles halftones, folds and die-cuts, multiple-page designs, and thematic expressions.

Beginning with chapter 3, exercises or design problems are listed at the end of each chapter along with our demonstrated examples. They can be attempted by the reader after reading through a chapter, or freely modified to suit specific levels of learning.

The authors are grateful to the Aldus Corporation, for providing the software programs Aldus FreeHand, Aldus SuperPaint, and Aldus PageMaker; the Adobe System, Inc., for providing Adobe Illustrator and Adobe PhotoShop; Letraset, for providing LetraStudio and the Slipstream font; and CE Software, for Amazing Paint. All of these programs have been used in the preparation of the diagrams, illustrations, and page layouts.

10

1

14

Generally speaking, design is the result of a kind of structured activity, representing a valid, efficient, cost-effective, and visually satisfying solution to a pre-established problem.

As such, design can be in two dimensions—drawn, painted, or printed on paper, fabric, or any type of flat surface. Or it can be in three dimensions—manufactured or assembled in any suitable material. A design can even form an environment by itself, incorporating light, sound, and probably also movement.

At one end, there is the functional aspect of design, which has to do with practical needs and the exacting demands of communication. Here, guided by business or other directives and restrained by budgets and production processes, the designer is a problem-solver and often works with other experts in a team.

At the other end, there is the visual aspect of design, which has to do with the creation and arrangement of shapes, patterns, and possibly textual elements, and the effects of their interrelationships. For this aspect—attaining a high standard of visual accomplishment—the designer always assumes full responsibility.

VISUAL DESIGN

Our prime objective is to present an analysis of the visual language used in design creation. The study of this visual language entails learning its vocabulary and grammar, and will lead to experiments in visual design.

We shall presently look into the various facets of visual design and examine various stages and methods of the actual designing process. Our demonstrations and suggested experiments for the reader will generally be limited to two-dimensional designs in black and white and grayscale that can be printed inexpensively on paper.

AESTHETIC ORGANIZATION

In most cases, visual design is no more than aesthetic organization.

Basic elements such as dots, lines, curves, squares, rectangles, triangles, polygons, circles, ellipses, letters, numbers, symbols, and so on, are often the ingredients of our shapes and compositions. These basic elements are not created by us, but we have to organize them to achieve satisfying visual results.

Aesthetic organization involves the choice of appropriate elements, as well as decisions concerning their specific dimensions, colors, shades, textures, and arrangement.

16

DECORATION

Some kinds of visual design, consisting of repeated motifs that accentuate, surround, or cover an entire surface, may be seen as decoration.

A decorative design must attract or please the eye and enhance the appearance of the surface it occupies.

Such a design can be a self-contained entity; a continuous band, border, or frame; a vignette; or an allover pattern.

The design may have cultural or historical references, if the motif comes from a particular source.

SELF-EXPRESSION

Visual design is not always decoration. As a form of self-expression it can convey a specific feeling, emotion, mood, or impression.

For instance, a geometric design might reflect the spirit of this technological era. Scattered fragments in a composition might suggest a mind searching for a new sense of order. Blurred shapes might suggest movement and speed.

As self-expression, the result or revelation of a highly individualistic endeavor, visual design can become art.

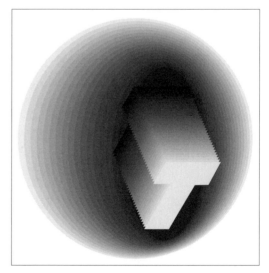

COMMUNICATION

Visual design can communicate a message when it incorporates words, symbols, or representational shapes readily understood by the viewer.

Words may have definite meanings. Symbols may have clear associations. Representational shapes may be based on physical objects and other phenomena. Abstract shapes that express feelings and emotions may also form part of visual communication.

When we deal with visual communication, our concern inevitably extends to the functional aspect of design.

THE DESIGNING PROCESS

Experiments in visual design may have no obvious commercial intent or any practical application, but they should not be purposeless.

Any design must start with a recognition of what is required by a given problem, and end with a valid solution to the problem. This process in turn requires systematic thinking, exploration of all possibilities, and proper decisions at right moments.

Prior to actual visualization and preparatory work for presentation, the designing process includes identification of the goal, interpretation of given specifications, preliminary research, development of ideas, finding methods, and planning of a working schedule.

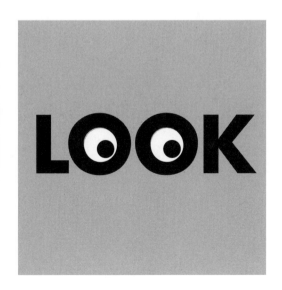

THE DESIGN PROBLEM

In visual design, a problem could be a simple exercise, such as recreating an existing shape or seeking its variations through demonstrated methods and techniques.

It could consist of a set of well-defined specifications, imposing rigid constraints on what is permissible or impermissible.

It could offer a range of choices, allowing wide latitude and encouraging unusual attempts.

It could also provide a theme, probably requiring some research, with an emphasis on expression and communication.

THE GOAL

Any design problem must have a goal. The goal might, for instance, relate to the development of design concepts or skills, or artistic sensitivity to a particular stage.

If a number of problems are interrelated, the separate goals of individual problems should be guided by a general goal.

In the progress of a course, actual statement of a the goal in a design problem may not be necessary as long as there is clear understanding of why the problem is set, what kind of effect the design should achieve, and what level of accomplishment should be attained.

SPECIFICATIONS

Specifications for a design usually form the core of
the design problem. These may include the overall
dimensions and quantity of work, elements to be
included, methods or techniques to be used, theme
or choice of themes, message to be conveyed,
preferences, restrictions, style of presentation, and
the due date.

All specifications must be strictly followed. They
determine what should be done and what should
not be done. They may allow for different interpre-
tations, however, and can be incomplete and
vague to provide room for individual explorations.

PRELIMINARY RESEARCH

Design problems that consist of simple exercises
with simple and straightforward specifications may
not require preliminary research work.

Problems that call for materials with social, historical, or cultural references, however, may mean
seeking out and finding and sorting the necessary
information. Such visual information could be
obtained from books or in visits to special locations.

Sometimes a problem may require research in the
technical area, such as finding out different kinds
of paper; methods of printing, folding, and binding;
and the availability of supply sources and services.

IDEAS AND METHODS

Preliminary research also includes browsing through design books and magazines, looking for examples of solutions to similar problems or for sources of inspiration. A designer should always be on the alert for new ideas and methods, and aware of current trends and rejuvenated styles.

Although straightforward imitation should be discouraged, imitation with modifications is often a part of the learning process. Ideas and methods do not germinate from nothing, after all, but are developed from or as reaction to existing ideas and methods.

There are several levels of formulation and implementation of ideas and methods during the designing process. On the conceptual level, we should seek a fresh approach to the problem. On the visual level, we attempt to create a unique composition. On the technical level, we look into the use of unusual material and processes in design production.

THE WORKING SCHEDULE

It is always a good practice to establish and adhere to a working schedule for any problem that is more than a simple exercise.

The working schedule is a constraining timetable, defining dates and times for preliminary research, visualization, and presentation to meet a deadline that cannot be postponed.

Work can be divided into stages, and the amount of time required for each stage can be estimated. The due date should be set as an absolute deadline.

VISUALIZATION

Ideas are nothing until we can see them as shapes, and so actual design starts with visualization. Several stages of visualization may be required for the ideas to take shape.

Initially, the ideas could be in crude sketchy shapes. Whatever comes to mind might be visualized, with no concern for details and proportions.

Selected rough visualizations might then be carried to the next stage for further development as more finished shapes or compositions.

At the final stage, one of the more finished shapes or compositions might be chosen as the best solution to the problem, and then be rendered in several variations, each of which will be given all possible refinement.

PRESENTATION

Presentation represents the conclusion of all design efforts, when the results of tackling a given problem are ready to be seen by other people.

For presentation, the design should be in a highly finished form. This requires printing the design on paper, along with some post-printing treatment such as trimming and mounting.

The design may require special cuts and folds as part of the post-printing treatment, but these should be well conceived during the various stages of visualization.

Although much of the work in presentation is of a technical nature, the full impact of a design can be significantly enhanced with good presentation.

EVALUATION

Whether a design is visually satisfying has much to do with subjective preferences. Evaluation of the same design as a valid solution to a particular problem, however, might be objective. The following is a list of questions that could help to establish a set of criteria:

- Has the design met the deadline?
- Does the design incorporate all given specifications?
- Does the design contain all necessary information?
- Did the designer understand the problem or reach the goal?
- Did the designer provide a unique solution to the problem?
- Has the design reached a high standard of visual accomplishment?
- Is there room for further improvement?

The above are arranged somewhat in a descending order of importance. All the questions reflect the discipline of the design profession and demand positive answers, although there are different levels of achievement in each case.

SETTING PROBLEMS

Most of the problems included in our book are only briefly described, usually with vague specifications. The self-learner or the teacher may wish to redefine the specifications, or to set different problems. The following checklist can be used as a guide whenever a specific problem needs to be set:

- The goal
- Specifications for subject matter or theme
- Specifications for information to be included
- Specifications for visual requirements
- Specifications for dimensional requirements
- Specifications for technical requirements
- Specifications for post-printing treatment
- Specifications for the procedural requirements
- Specifications for quantity and range of work
- Suggestions and preferences
- Evaluation criteria
- The deadline

2

In conventional practice, visual design may be sketched, drawn, or painted on paper or cardboard. The tools used include pencil, marker, pen with ink, brushes with paint, and airbrush with liquid color, along with drawing board, T-square, protractor, ruler, triangles, compasses, French curves, and flexible curve-guides.

This method has distinct advantages, for we are dealing with actual tools, along with physical materials and media, and the shapes created have a tactile presence. In addition, we can improve our drawing abilities as we develop our design skills.

The conventional method also has disadvantages. The accurate rendering and arrangement of shapes can be extremely time consuming. Any change might call for a major revision. Less work is accomplished with greater effort, and the entire process—the attainment of finished work—is slow.

Now most of such visualization work can be done on the computer with comparable or even better results. The computer not only offers efficiency and precision, it also opens a new horizon in visual creation. It makes learning visual design easier within a much shorter time span.

THE COMPUTER REVOLUTION

The computer is a machine that works with electronic signals. It was first invented to calculate
complex figures and formulas and to sort data.
Later developments in computer technology vastly
extended its capabilities, making the computer useful for all kinds of human needs and enabling the
machine to complete otherwise tedious manual
tasks quickly, easily, and reliably.

Formerly occupying an entire room, the computer
has shrunk drastically in size over the decades. Its
price has also decreased to the extent that the
computer has gradually become standard equipment in offices and homes.

THE NEW VISUAL LANGUAGE

Understanding the computer and working with it
effectively require a thorough acquaintance with its
special language, and computer language, in its
full technical range, can be very complex.

For a general user who does not do programming,
computer language is no more than a set of simple
rules and commands employed to achieve specific
results.

For the designer, this language primarily comprises
methods and procedures for originating lines,
shapes, and type. Such elements, in desired colors,
shades, and patterns, are available to us at the
click of a finger or with slight movement of the
palm, and their alignment, distribution, duplication,
and transformation can be done almost instantly.

We are now dealing with a new visual language—
with which our traditional principles of design may
have to be completely redefined.

COMPUTER HARDWARE

To tackle this new visual language, we need to become acquainted with computer equipment which we may have to acquire on our own.

Computer equipment falls into two main systems. There are the IBM-compatibles (generally referred to as the PCs), made by many manufacturers. There are also the Macintoshes, manufactured solely by Apple Computers, Inc.

Differences between the two systems are gradually narrowing and may soon be completely eliminated. At this point the Macintoshes—which introduced the graphical user interface that enables the user to operate directly with simple visual displays—are still favored by people in the design industry.

A computer for design use should have a RAM (random access memory) of 5 or more megabytes in its central processing unit, with a built-in hard drive providing storage of 80 or more megabytes. Megabyte is the unit of memory measurement, an indication of the computer's working capacity.

The only other piece of equipment needed for a modest start is a laser printer that can work with *PostScript*, a page-description language developed by Adobe Systems, Inc., for high-resolution printing. A hand-held or flat-bed scanner could be obtained as the need arises.

COMPUTER SOFTWARE

A computer cannot accomplish anything without relevant software. Software refers to programs pre-recorded on *floppy disks* for installation into the computer's internal memory storage or any external hard drive connected to it.

Different programs serve different purposes. Word-processing, spreadsheet, and database programs satisfy the needs of most people. Graphics programs are used by designers.

Graphics programs generally fall into several classifications: draw, paint, image editing, page layout, font creation and manipulation, and three-dimensional rendering.

A program always comes with a manual that explains the techniques and procedures particular to the program. A tutorial book with a step-by-step guide to help the user might also be part of the program package.

THE MONITOR SCREEN

On most computers today the *central processing unit* is separate from the other components, which are all detachable. Standard components sold in an integrated package can be exchanged for more desirable components, and be replaced at any time.

The most conspicuous component is the *monitor*, which usually sits on top of the central processing unit. The function of the monitor is to display information and visual images on a *screen* in grayscale or full color.

As the computer is started, in most circumstances, the lit screen contains a *menu bar* at the top, and a largely blank space that represents the *desktop* with an array of *icons*. Icons are symbols representing the disk drives, programs, folders, files, or documents available for use.

After a program is launched, a *document window* shows up on the desktop, functioning as a piece of paper for image creation and display. The startup menu bar changes to one associated with the program. This consists of a row of *menu heads*, each containing a list of *commands* for specific tasks.

THE KEYBOARD

Another essential component directly connected to the central processing unit is the *keyboard,* which is the main input device in computer operation.

A computer keyboard is similar to that of a typewriter, with almost identical rows of keys for typing characters, as well as some additional keys.

There are the *Command* and *Option* keys for effecting shortcuts and changes, and a set of four arrow keys for moving a cursor or selected element on screen. A numerical pad may be present for entering numbers, calculation work, and other functions. An extended keyboard also contains a row of function keys for expedited commands.

THE MOUSE

Another input device is the *mouse*, a small, movable, palm-sized unit with a cable linked to the keyboard.

A standard mouse has a ball underneath its casing and a button at the top that can be depressed. Moving the mouse on a rubber or vinyl pad rolls the ball and transports a cursor on screen. The cursor represents the location and tracking of the mouse.

Generally, the mouse cursor is used for insertion of text and for selection of commands from the menu bar. In a draw or paint program, the mouse cursor can represent pencil, pen, or brush. It also selects and moves elements and shapes, as well as modifies and transforms them.

The mouse is used either by *clicking*, which means momentarily depressing and releasing the mouse button, or by *dragging*, which means firmly holding down its button while moving the mouse on the soft pad. The two ways serve different purposes.

TOOLBOX AND PALETTE

The mouse cursor frequently takes an arrow shape to access commands in all programs and to select a particular *tool* in a *toolbox*.

The toolbox is a compartmentalized rectangular box displayed on screen and containing pictorial symbols, each of which represents a special tool for drawing, painting, or image manipulation.

After a tool is clicked on, the cursor changes shape, indicating that it is ready for performing the work specific to the tool.

A tool may be associated with a *palette* on display. A palette is in the shape of a narrow strip or box, showing a range of options, such as shades, colors, patterns, textures, or just a list of descriptive words. How a tool works is affected by the option chosen in the palette.

DIALOG BOX AND INFORMATION BAR

Selecting a command under a menu head, or double clicking on a tool in the toolbox, may activate the display of a *dialog box*, which offers further choices and facilitates numerical entries for precise operations.

An *information bar* can be on constant display to show the coordinates of the mouse cursor, or locations, measurements, angles, and movements of one selected element or shape. This becomes a *control bar* if it functions like a palette or dialog box, providing options and making possible instant changes.

DRAW PROGRAMS

To draw is to visualize primarily with thin lines, which can then become edges of shapes. In a draw program, the lines are generally straight or smoothly curved, although some irregularity may be introduced. They are always sharply defined and never blurred, but can be broad or fine and in dark or light shades.

A draw program is object oriented, which means each element or shape is a separable object that can be individually selected for moving, changing, or deleting. Elements or shapes can be joined and split, grouped and ungrouped, anytime in the drawing process. They are piled up as layers that can be reshuffled, temporarily hidden from view, or withheld from printing.

A full-featured draw program allows precise control of lengths, sizes, positions, and directions, and also facilitates changes in line weights, filling with colors and patterns, instantaneous repetitions and sequential duplications, transformations and blends, and elaborate manipulation of type and lines of text. It contains rulers, guides, information bars, and probably also a built-in grid for manual or automatic alignment.

PAINT PROGRAMS

Paint programs were designed to simulate the intuitive way we sketch and paint. What is created on screen are images composed of affected minute picture elements, or *pixels*, which have been changed from the white of the screen to black, gray, or color by the dragging of a mouse cursor representing one of the paint tools.

Each pixel stands for a *bit*, a unit making up the monitor screen's normal resolution of 72 dpi (dots per inch). A paint image is often referred to as *bit-mapped*, as it is mapped out by affected bits.

Operation of a paint tool produces a mark on screen that immediately fuses with any previous mark it overlaps, and is fused by any subsequent marks that lie on top of it. All fused marks are inseparable, except by undoing with a command immediately after the mouse operation. Correction is achieved by erasing, or overpainting with white.

Earlier versions of paint programs that work only in black and white produce rather crude results. Later versions that work in grayscale and full color are worthy of serious jobs.

IMAGE-EDITING PROGRAMS

Image-editing programs are for retouching, modifying, and transforming photographs that are brought to the computer screen with a scanner or some other device.

Scanning, however, is not limited to photographs but includes all two-dimensional shapes sketched, painted, or printed on a flat surface.

A scanner usually comes with its own program for image editing. As scanned images are bit-mapped, image editing can also be done in most paint programs.

Highly technical work still requires a specialized program that offers more extensive and exacting control.

PAGE-LAYOUT PROGRAMS

A page-layout program imports pictorial and typographical elements from other programs and organizes them on one page or in a sequence of pages.

Pictorial elements, such as illustrations and photographs from draw, paint, or image-editing programs, can be rescaled, cropped, masked, framed, or given new backgrounds. Typographical elements, such as headlines and texts originated with word-processing programs, can be edited, given font, size, style, and justification changes, constrained in specially shaped text boxes, framed with lines, and shifted to wrap around pictorial elements.

Page-layout programs are indispensable in desktop publishing work dealing with large amounts of text in multiple pages.

OTHER GRAPHICS PROGRAMS

Some programs are for the creation of customized typefaces, their modification, transformation, and distortion.

Some can turn flat type and shapes into three-dimensional images, which can be rotated in space away from frontality.

Some can create perspective views of objects, with light and shadow modeling to create an illusion of reality.

Some provide unusual effects with textures and shapes and colors.

These programs serve very specialized purposes and are supplementary to the main graphics programs.

CHOICE OF PROGRAMS

A program should be acquired only when there is a real, immediate need for it. It is unwise to acquire a program for future use. All programs are periodically upgraded by their manufacturers, and new versions may make older versions obsolete.

Choice of program depends on what features answer the most essential needs, its compatibility with existing equipment, and its interface with other programs. Some programs may seem easy to use but lack real power, whereas others may demand considerable effort to master.

Working with concepts described in our book frequently requires one full-featured draw program. There are many draw programs on the market, but the real choice is probably between Aldus FreeHand, from Aldus Corporation, and Adobe Illustrator, from Adobe Systems, Inc., both having similar features but different strengths and weaknesses.

Adobe Illustrator has more type-manipulation capabilities and includes special tools for chart making. Aldus FreeHand offers greater control for formal organization, with grids and guides for snapping elements into definite positions.

As we deal generally with the orderly arrangement of elements and shapes, we use Aldus FreeHand far more often than Adobe Illustrator, although both are equally desirable. Thus our descriptions of technical procedures are based largely on Aldus FreeHand. The terms we use may have come from different programs.

Instead of a program exclusively for painting, our preference is for a combined paint/draw program, which provides flexibility in transferring painted and drawn results. Our choice here is Aldus SuperPaint, from Aldus Corporation. One of its unique features is the creation of "SuperBits" to improve the resolution of bit-mapped images. Its draw capabilities almost make it an all-purpose program for our basic graphic needs.

For image editing, Adobe PhotoShop, from Adobe Systems, Inc., is unquestionably the ultimate choice. It can do color and grayscale painting and offers numerous filters for image transformation.

Aldus PageMaker, also from Aldus Corporation, has been used for all the page layouts of this book. Its extensive features are even further enhanced with a recent update. In addition, LetraStudio (from Letraset), which distorts both type and graphics, meets occasional needs. These programs may be worth considering once you have attained greater proficiency on the computer.

3

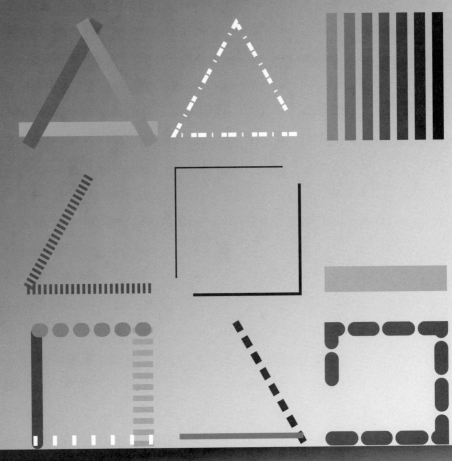

3 4

We can start our first experiments in visual design by working with straight lines in a draw program.

A straight line is the simplest element in graphics. It links and represents the shortest distance between two points, each being an *end point* if the line is not subsequently connected to another line.

End points anchor the starting and terminating locations of the straight line on screen, and determine its length, position, and direction in space.

The line is visible to us because it has visual attributes, which include weight, color, shade, pattern, and texture.

In a draw program, we can make a straight line by dragging, with the mouse cursor representing the *line tool* in the toolbox, or by clicking, with the mouse cursor representing the *corner tool* or the *pen tool*.

Names of tools, terms, methods, and procedures, however, vary considerably with different programs. The user should always have the program manual available for constant reference.

END POINTS AND LENGTH

End points marking the beginning and the end of a line are indicated by solid or hollow square dots as the line is made (**A**). Their presence informs us that the line is *selected* and ready for the next operation.

The straight line initially appears in black on screen. Its length in inches or some other units of measurement can be seen in an information bar. We can get vertical and horizontal rulers on display to determine length and to guide positioning.

Clicking with the mouse cursor representing the *arrow tool,* a general-purpose selection tool in the toolbox, can *deselect* the line and hide the end points. Clicking again with the mouse cursor on the line again reselects it, and we can click further on one of the end points and drag to extend its length (**B**) or even change its direction (**C**).

We can move a selected line by dragging, with the arrow tool touching the body of the line between end points. We can also press an arrow key on the keyboard to effect pixel-by-pixel movement of any selected line or point.

DIRECTION OF A LINE

The straight line is in a horizontal direction if its end points are equidistant from the upper or lower edge of the document window (**D**). It is in a vertical direction if its end points are equidistant from the left or right edge of the window (**E**).

Vertical and horizontal directions are the basic directions. We can depress the Shift key on the keyboard as we drag with the line tool to get lines in such directions. The Shift key actually constrains lines in 45-degree-angle increments (**F**).

A horizontal line is at 0 degrees. A vertical line is at 90 degrees. Although we can change the direction of a line by moving one of its end points, a proper way of doing this is to use the *rotating tool,* monitoring the angle of rotation with reference to the information bar, or specifying the desired angle in an associated dialog box, with positive figures representing anticlockwise rotation and negative figures representing clockwise rotation. Using the rotating tool to change the direction of a line maintains the line's original length.

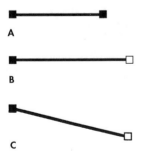

A

B

C

D

E

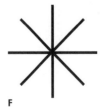

F

WEIGHT OF A LINE

The weight of a line is gauged in terms of *points* or fractions of points, which are units of measurement traditionally used in the printing industry and remain commonly adopted. There are 72 points to an inch.

The finest line that can be produced with the computer is a *hairline,* which has the weight of a quarter of a point (**A**). We can have half-point lines and lines ranging from 1 point to 72 or more in thickness. A one-inch line with a weight of 72 points has a square shape (**B**).

By default, upon creation a line may have a one-point weight. We can change its weight immediately, or do this later.

The program may allow us to work both in the *keyline* and the *preview* modes. While the preview mode is often preferable, the keyline mode is useful for precise positioning, since all lines will appear as fine lines regardless of their assigned weights.

A design can be conceived with lines alone, for lines can be regarded as planar shapes when their weights are significant (**C**).

COLOR/SHADE OF A LINE

In addition to weight, other attributes of a line include color, shade, pattern, configuration of its ends, and characteristics of its body. All these can be specially assigned and changed.

A color palette is often available for color and shade attributes. As we will not work in color, we shall restrict this discussion to gray shades or black. The palette normally provides a range of commonly used shades in percentages of black and allows the addition of special shades.

Lines stroked with a shade are always opaque. A black line can be obstructed by a light gray line on top of it (**D**). A number of closely positioned lines stroked in gradually varying gray shades can form a plane showing smooth steps of tonal transition (**E**).

All lines will be in black when we switch to the keyline mode.

A

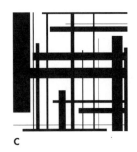

B

C

D

E

PATTERN OF A LINE

Assigning attributes to a line is to *stroke* it. We can have the line in black or in an evenly tinted shade, but we can also have it in a pattern, which is an option provided in the dialog box or palette for attributes.

Patterns are bit-mapped, often in a 72-dpi resolution regardless of the printer used. An assortment of stock patterns is usually available, and each pattern can be edited. The whites in a pattern are usually opaque. All patterns remain in the same direction and size, independent of the direction and weight of the line (**A**).

Patterns are effective with broad lines only. A thin line can appear broken when patterned. A design with broad lines stroked with many shades and patterns may not reveal that it was constructed of lines (**B**).

CAPS AND ARROWHEADS

The two ends of a line usually appear squared, with no additional caps. These squared ends are referred to as *butt caps* and do not extend the line's length (**C**).

In the dialog box for attributes, we can pick the *square cap* option. The line maintains its squared end, but is lengthened at each end by a cap equal to half of its weight (**D**). We can also choose the *round cap* option, which also extends the line's length (**E**).

An option for arrowheads may be available (**F**). Arrowheads are special caps with prominent shapes that extend the line's length considerably.

Caps and arrowheads increase proportionately in size with increase of the line weight (**G**) and always have the same attributes as the main body of the line (**H**). They add variety in a design where lines exclusively are used (**I**).

3 7

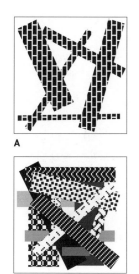

A

B

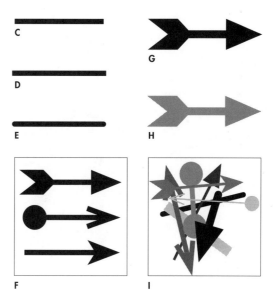

C

D

E

F

G

H

I

JOINS

DASHES

Two straight lines can be connected at their end points. This is accomplished with the *join elements* command after moving an end point of one line to coincide with an end point of another (**A**).

The result is a crooked line. We can also get a crooked line by extending an existing straight line in a direction different from its original direction. This can be accomplished by clicking with the *corner tool* to establish a new end point after selecting one end point of the line. Clicking several times can create an angular line with many intermediate points (**B**).

The line now consists of *segments* that are linked together. At each junction of adjacent segments is a *join*, which may bend inward or outward. Joins can be in specific shapes. We can choose from the dialog box for such attributes as a *miter join*, for sharp protrusion (**C**), a *round join*, for smooth protrusion (**D**), or a *beveled join*, for truncated protrusion (**E**). A miter join can become truncated if the angle for *miter limit* is larger than the angle of the join.

There is also a *dash* option for stroking the line. This breaks up the body of the line.

Dashes are short strokes replacing the continuous line. Stock dash patterns are available, but we can determine stroke lengths and widths of intervening gaps (**F**), and can specify caps that may narrow or partially close the gaps. Rectangular or square dashes can become oval dots when round caps are in effect (**G**).

Dashes can be in any line weight and gray shade. A broad line composed of very short dashes and narrow gaps would appear in a pattern of parallel lines (**H**). Dash patterns, however, always rotate with the line, and gaps are transparent (**I**).

An angular line can be changed to dashes. We should choose the beveled join option to avoid having prominent solid joins (**J**).

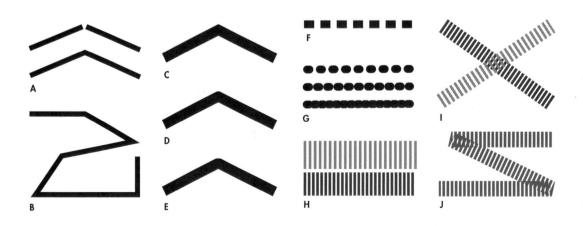

A   B   C   D   E   F   G   H   I   J

DUPLICATING A LINE

A selected line may be cloned with the *clone* command. Cloning places an exact copy right on top of the original. The copy then becomes selected and can be moved with the arrow tool or with arrow keys to a new location.

With the moved copy remaining selected, we can activate the *duplicate* command, as many times as desired, to obtain further copies (with identical position changes), which will be automatically arranged in a definite order (**A**).

The process is called *power duplication*, and is very useful in many situations. For instance, if a cloned copy is moved and then rotated, power duplication can produce a series of subsequent copies with progressive rotation (**B**).

Without prior cloning, the duplicate command will just produce a copy of the selected line and place it slightly offset toward the lower right corner of the original. More copies can be obtained in the same way (**C**).

We can also use the *copy* command to place a copy of a selected line in the computer's *clipboard*, which simply stores what is most recently copied. After copying, we can use the *paste* command to place a copy of the line from the clipboard at the center of the document window, and can have any number of copies of the same line later if the content of the clipboard is not changed.

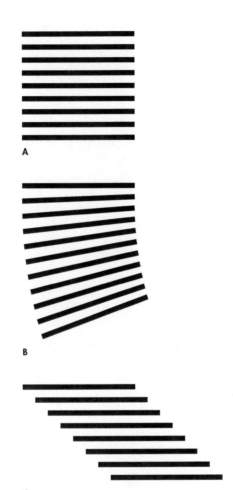

A

B

C

WHITE LINES

The color palette contains not only a range of gray shades in varying percentages of black, but also a "none" and a "white" option. Choosing "none" will remove a selected line from display in the preview mode, but it is still there and can be located if we switch to the keyline mode. Choosing "white" may also lead to the disappearance of the selected line, but the selected line then becomes visible if placed in front of any line, shape, or background that is not white.

We can obtain a two-layer line by first stroking a broad line in black and extending it with square or round caps. After cloning it, we can stroke the copy as a thin white line, which forms a slit along the main body of the original broad line (**A**).

Repeating this process with alternating black and white stroking and with gradual decrease of line weights can produce a multi-layer line composed of concentric lines surrounding a single black or white line at the center (**B**).

We can group this multi-layer line with a *group* command and obtain copies arranged in a parallel direction (**C**) or various directions (**D**).

A number of white lines can be laid on top of one extremely broad black or gray line to slice it into separate portions (**E**).

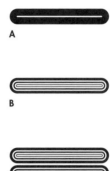

A

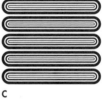

B

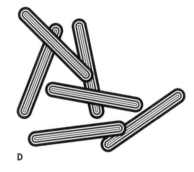

C

D

E

INTERSECTING LINES

Two straight lines in different directions can intersect one another only at a point.

If both lines are stroked black or with the same gray shade or pattern, they seem fused together (**A**).

If they are of different grays or patterns, or one in solid black, the other in gray or in a pattern, then the most recently created line appears on top of the one created earlier (**B**).

A *send to front* command can bring forward a selected line at the back. Alternatively, we can use a *send to back* command to push a selected line behind (**C**).

Working exclusively in black and white, we can create a white line, say about 12 points in weight, in any desirable length, with square caps, and subsequently clone it with attributes of solid black, a 10-point weight, and the same caps. The two-layer line can be grouped as one entity, duplicated, and rotated for intersecting arrangements. Each copy of the two-layer line will have a thin white border for distinguishing it from others (**D**).

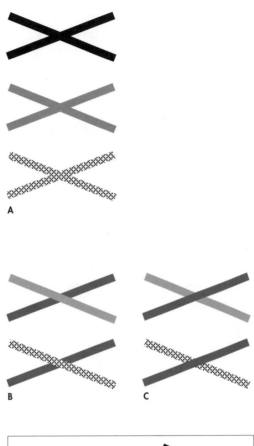

A

B   C

D

BLENDING LINES

42

We can select one line with the arrow key, and further select one of its end points by just clicking on the point. We can hold down the Shift key to *co-select* another line, and further select one of the end points of that line.

With two lines selected, and with an end point of each line correspondingly further selected, we can blend the two lines with a *blend* command, which opens a dialog box allowing us to obtain any number of intermediate steps. If both lines are parallel and identical in length and attributes, all intermediate steps are just repeats, parallel to and equidistant from one another (**A**).

The original and intermediate lines now form a group. Holding down the Option key, we can use the arrow tool to *subselect* one of the original lines, further selecting an end point if necessary, and move the entire line or just the point. Any moving can cause the group to reblend in a new configuration (**B**).

If the subselected line is lengthened, shortened, or slanted, all intermediate lines in the group will automatically adjust their lengths or directions in a sequence (**C**, **D**). If it is reassigned a heavier line weight or a different shade, the blend will reflect such changes (**E**, **F**).

A straight line may be blended with an angular line that has one or more joins. The blend will show the straight line progressively bending to approach the configuration of the angular line (**G**).

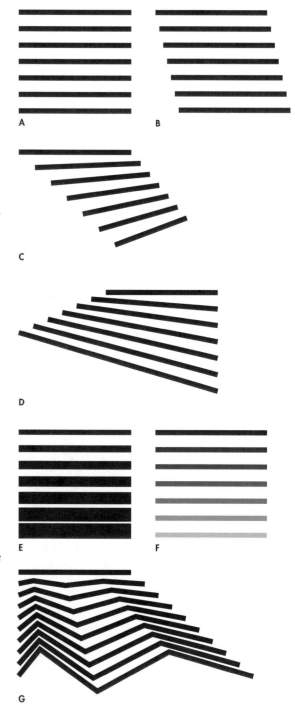

A   B

C

D

E   F

G

SUGGESTED PROBLEMS

Try creating two similar angular lines of different gray shades and blend them to obtain a number of steps (**A**). Subsequently try subselecting one original line to change its position (**B**), direction (**C**), line weight (**D**), and configuration (**E**).

The blended group can be ungrouped. After ungrouping, try rearranging the lines freely, rotating, and assigning new attributes to some if necessary, so that they no longer reflect the sequential order of the blend (**F** - **I**).

A

B

C

D

E

4 4

F

H

G

I

4

46

Although broad straight lines of short lengths are regarded as shapes, shape can be defined as a plane enclosed within a continuous, confining edge.

Rectangles and ellipses are two very basic shapes from which many other shapes can be developed, and *shape tools* enable us to create these shapes on the computer.

In any draw program, we can find a *rectangle tool* for making rectangles and squares, an *ellipse tool* for making ellipses and circles, and usually also a *rounded-rectangle tool* for making rectangles and squares with rounded corners.

When a shape first appears on screen, it is usually shown in an outlined form, to which desired attributes can be subsequently assigned. In the keyline mode, all shapes will always be displayed as outlines again regardless of their attributes.

RECTANGLES AND SQUARES

With the mouse cursor representing the rectangle tool, we can drag diagonally across the screen, starting from one upper corner and moving to the opposite lower corner, to make a rectangle with two equal vertical sides and two equal horizontal sides.

This rectangle can be so narrow and elongated that it is seen as a line (**A**), or have all equal sides and become a square (**B**). To attain a perfect square (its width and height can be read on the information bar), we can depress the Shift key as we drag with the tool cursor.

The rectangle or square comes as a grouped shape, marked with four tiny square dots at its four corners when it remains selected (**C**). These dots are *object handles*. Moving any object handle with the arrow tool can change the shape's size and/or proportion without affecting its orientation.

The grouped rectangle or square actually has a center, which is marked with an "x" shape in the keyline mode (**D**). We can originate a rectangle or square from any particular point, with that point as the center of the figure, by holding down the Option key before dragging.

ROUNDED RECTANGLES OR SQUARES

Rectangles or squares can have rounded corners if we choose the *rounded-rectangle tool* instead of the standard rectangle tool. A dialog box associated with the tool facilitates changing or specifying the corner radius (**E**, **F**).

We can enter a radius value large enough to create a rectangle approaching an ellipse (**G**) or a square approaching a circle (**H**). A suitable radius value can enable us to create elongated shapes with two rounded ends (**I**).

Dragging any handle of a selected rounded square or rectangle can change the shape's size and proportion without affecting the roundness of its corners (**J**).

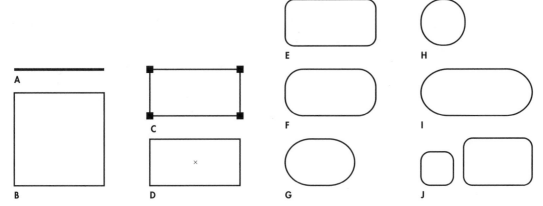

A

B

C

D

E

F

G

H

I

J

ELLIPSES AND CIRCLES

Drawing an ellipse was once a difficult task. Now we can always create one in a perfect configuration with one simple mouse movement. Operations of the ellipse tool are similar to those of the rectangle tool. Dragging the tool cursor with the Option key depressed creates the shape from the center. Dragging while holding down the Shift key creates a perfect circle.

The shape, as it remains selected, also has four black square dots representing the object handles (**A**, **B**). We can change its size and proportion by moving any object handle with the arrow tool.

The ellipse has a height different from its width and shows a definite orientation. A circle with a constant radius or diameter has no particular orientation. Both are bordered with a continuous, smooth curve, which winds toward only one direction.

ASSIGNING ATTRIBUTES

Any rectangle, square, ellipse, or circle has an outline that can be stroked and an enclosed plane that can be filled.

As we assign attributes, we can stroke the outline as we would any independent line, with a choice of line weight, shade, and pattern (**C**), as well as choice of dashes and caps for the dashes (**D**). For a rectangle or square, there is also the choice of joins (**E**).

We can *fill* the enclosed plane, with a choice of shade and pattern (**F**). We can have gradient (**G**) or radial fills (**H**) if desired.

Stroke and fill for the shape can be in any combination (**I**). If these are in the same shade or pattern, the shape may appear slightly larger than it should be when the weight of the outline is significant (**J**).

We can stroke or fill the shape in "white" or "none," effects of which will be discussed later.

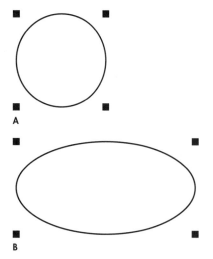

A
B

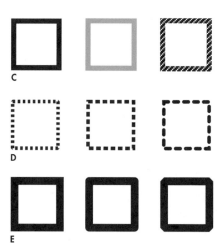

C
D
E

NEGATIVE SHAPES

If we stroke and fill a shape with white (**K**, **L**), or fill it with white without stroking it (**M**, **N**), we can use it as a negative shape to cut out a portion or make a hole in any visible shape.

If we stroke the shape with white without filling it, then it will "carve" a negative linear shape in any visible shape it overlaps (**O**, **P**).

F

G

H

I

J

K

L

M

N

O

P

OVERLAPPING SHAPES

Two overlapping shapes that are both stroked and filled with the same flat shade or pattern, or stroked "none" but filled the same way, simply fuse with one another indistinguishably (**A**).

If the front shape is stroked with a shade, pattern, or just white, it becomes visually distinct from the shape it overlaps (**B**, **C**). If it is stroked with a shade or pattern, but filled with white, the white opaquely covers what is behind it (**D**, **E**). If we change the fill from white to "none," the enclosed plane becomes transparent, allowing anything behind it to be seen (**F**). If the front shape is stroked with white but filled with "none," it effects a negative line on the shape behind (**G**).

When there are more than two shapes overlapping, we can have the front or the in-between shape stroked with "none" but filled with white, to create negative effects (**H**, **I**).

JOINING SHAPES

Two overlapping shapes can be *joined*. Joining means that the two shapes become a *composite* shape, with the two shapes fully integrated.

To attain joining, each shape must be first ungrouped with the *ungroup* command, as rectangles and ellipses are grouped shapes. Then, after being selected, the shapes can be joined with the *join elements* command .

The composite shape representing the two joined shapes will contain a transparent *hole* where overlapping occurs (**J**).

We can join three or more overlapping shapes, with holes showing alternately in the overlapping areas (**K**).

After joining, all strokes and fills of the shapes will conform to attributes assigned to the shape of the farthest back layer. We can, if desired, give the composite shape a new set of attributes (**L**).

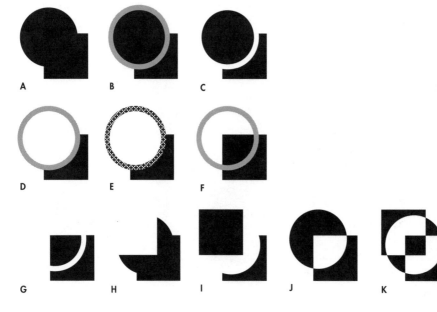

A   B   C

D   E   F

G   H   I   J   K   L

SCALING SHAPES

As mentioned earlier, moving an object handle can change the size or proportion of a grouped shape. There is a *scaling tool* in the toolbox, associated with a dialog box, for resizing or changing proportions with greater control.

We can enlarge or reduce a shape with proportionate scaling (**A**), or disproportionate scaling, with different percentages for vertical and horizontal dimensions (**B**, **C**). The dialog box also provides options for corresponding scaling of the line weight (**D**) or for leaving it unaffected.

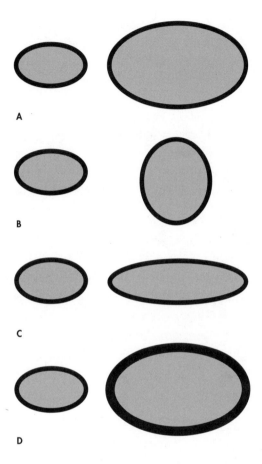

A

B

C

D

ROTATING SHAPES

52

We can use the rotating tool to rotate any selected shape. Clicking with the tool cursor places an invisible center of rotation on screen. The cursor can then be moved, acting as a lever, to effect rotation. The information bar will show the angle of rotation, as negative or positive figures, depending on whether the rotation is clockwise or anti-clockwise.

We can also rotate the shape by entering the angle in a dialog box associated with the tool, and we can choose either the shape's center or the cursor's clicked location as the center of rotation.

The selected shape can be cloned before rotation starts. After it is first rotated, we can use the duplicate command to effect power duplication, which produces further rotated copies.

If the shape's center is used as the center of rotation, all duplicated copies will overlap one another in a sequence (**A**). If the cursor's clicked location is used as the center of rotation, effects will vary according to where clicking occurred (**B**, **C**).

If the shape was originally stroked with an outline, the latest duplicated copy will remain visibly on top (**D**). The outlines can be removed so that all the shapes can fuse with one another (**E**). The shapes, with or without outlines, can be joined to become one composite shape (**F**).

A

B

C

D

E

F

REFLECTING SHAPES

There is a *reflecting tool* for changing a shape into its mirror image. Reflection is along an invisible, horizontal or vertical axis, but can be along a 45-degree or any angular axis.

The circle produces no distinguishably different look with reflection (**A**). The rectangle, the square, and the ellipse are all symmetrical shapes, and they must be reflected along an angular axis to show a different look (**B – D**), or reflected after they have angularly rotated (**E – G**). Placement and angle of the invisible axis can be determined by using the associated dialog box.

Prior cloning of the selected shape before reflection is necessary for achieving a new, bilaterally symmetrical shape composed of both the original and the reflected copy.

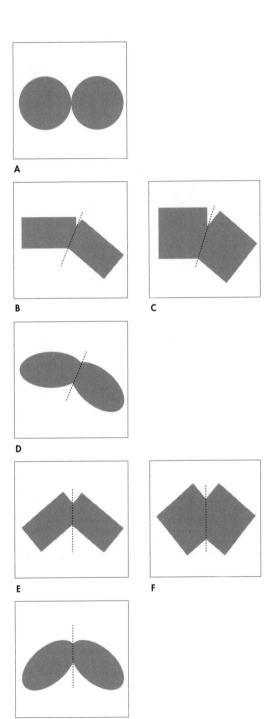

A

B

C

D

E

F

G

SKEWING SHAPES

54

To skew a shape is to transform it in a diagonal direction. This is accomplished with a *skewing tool* in the toolbox.

A rectangle (**A**) or square can be skewed to form a parallelogram or a rhombic shape. We can slant its vertical sides (**B**), its horizontal sides (**C**), or both vertical and horizontal sides (**D**), at an angle that can be read from the information bar. We can use the associated dialog box to determine how the shape should be skewed. The shape can be stretched or compressed in extreme cases of skewing (**E**, **F**).

An ellipse (**G**) or circle can also be skewed to become a slanting ellipse (**H**).

Cloning a shape before skewing produces a skewed copy on the baseline of the original. We can shift the first copy to a proper position and subsequently use power duplication to obtain a series of progressively skewed shapes overlapping one another (**I**).

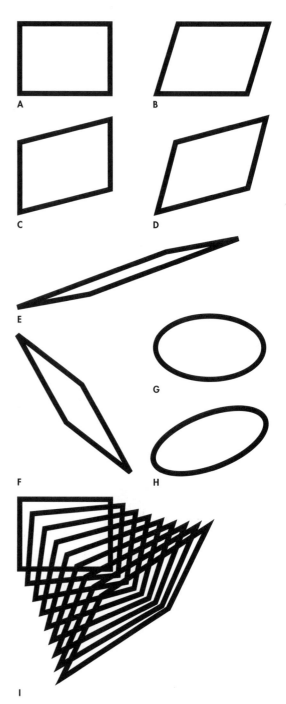

BLENDING SHAPES

Two shapes may be blended in any number of
intermediate steps. After selecting and ungrouping
them, we can proceed to select, by depressing the
Shift key, one corresponding point on each shape.
If the two shapes are exactly the same, blending
produces all intermediate shapes as exact copies of
the originals in an orderly arrangement (**A**).

For obvious blending effects showing progressive
changes, the starting and the terminating shape
may be of the same configuration but in different
line weights (**B**), shades of strokes (**C**), shades of
fills (**D**), sizes (**E**), directions (**F**), and/or skewed
transformations (**G**). They can also be in different
configurations (**H**). One smaller shape can be
placed in front but nested inside a larger shape in
blending (**I**).

After blending, we can subselect either the starting
or the terminating shape, using the arrow tool with
Option key depressed, and make changes, in the
same way we modify a blend of lines (see the section in chapter 3 on blending lines, page 42).

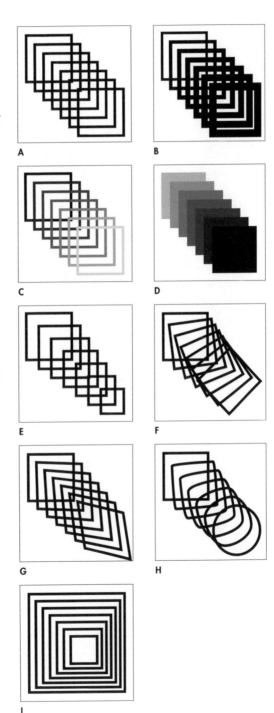

A

B

C

D

E

F

G

H

I

FINDING OPTIONS

56

The accompanying diagrams demonstrate how we can use a square shape to obtain a number of different configurations:

- Stroking the shape with a prominent line weight with no fill (**A**).
- Rounding the squared corners (**B**).
- Stroking and filling the shape with different percentages of black (**C**).
- Stroking and filling the shape with different patterns (**D**).
- Stroking and filling the shape with solid black, specifying round joins for the strokes (**E**).
- Filling the shape with a pattern without stroking, or stroking and filling it with the same pattern (**F**)
- Filling the shape with black without stroking. Subsequently cloning it and scaling the copy smaller with a new fill of white (**G**).
- Rotating the white shape (**H**).

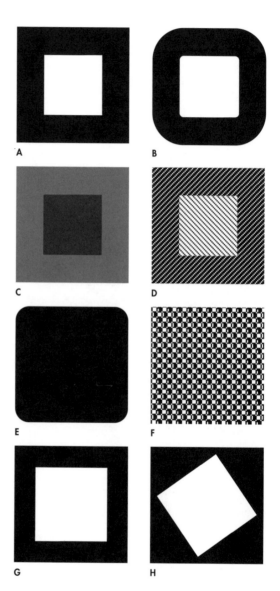

A

B

C

D

E

F

G

H

- Skewing the white shape (**I**).
- Reflecting the skewed white shape (**J**).
- Duplicating the white shape and shifting the copy towards lower right (**K**).
- Refilling the white shape in solid black (**L**).
- Ungrouping all shapes and joining them into one composite shape (**M**).
- Selecting the white shape in **H**, and stroking it in white with no fill. Subsequently cloning it, rotating the copy 45 degrees, and using power duplication to obtain a full revolution of the white-stroked shapes (**N**).
- Cloning a reduced, white-stroked shape on the larger black shape in the background, skewing it, and using power duplication to obtain more skewed copies. Subsequently cloning and rotating the entire group of white-stroked shapes 180 degrees (**O**).
- Cloning and rotating one white-stroked shape 45 degrees. Restroking the copy in dark gray while sending it to the back, and sending the background black shape even further back. Selecting and ungrouping the two outlined shapes. Subsequently blending them in four intermediate steps (**P**).

Adjustment of sizes and positions may be necessary in some cases.

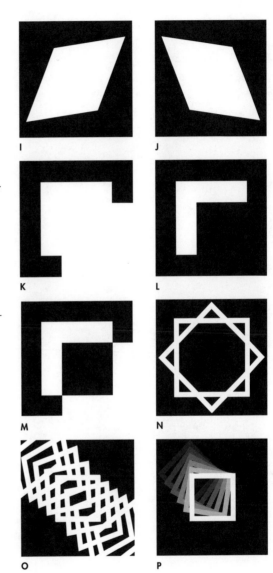

SUGGESTED PROBLEMS

58   Try arranging a number of rectangles and ellipses, as well as squares and circles, in various sizes, with similar or different attributes, with a lot of overlapping (**A**). Then try selecting all of them and join them into one composite shape (**B**). After joining, further try subselecting one component shape at a time and moving it, to change its general configuration (**C**).

B

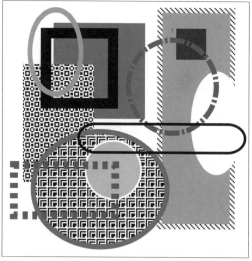

A

C

60   A straight line has two end points. An angular line has intermediate points at the joins between the end points.

A rectangle, square, ellipse, or circle, any group of newly blended lines or shapes, or a composite shape as a joined object, all come with four object handles, which are replaced with *points* upon ungrouping or upon subselection with the arrow tool.

All such points anchor the line or shape at specific locations with reference to the horizontal x-axis and the vertical y-axis of the window. They become visible on screen as the line or shape is selected.

Between any two adjacent points is a *path* or one segment of a path. Paths can be open or closed. An *open path* forms the basis of a line. A *closed path* forms the basis of a shape.

A closed path can be stroked as well as filled. An open path can be stroked, but normally is not filled and cannot be filled. Some programs can fill an open path by automatically connecting its end points with a straight edge to contain the fill.

CORNER POINTS

Points not only determine measurements and configurations of lines and shapes, but also affect any
segments relating to it. There are several types of
points. *Corner points* are probably the most common, as they are found on all the lines and shapes
discussed in chapters 3 and 4. These points act like
hinges at joins of segments.

Dragging with the line tool places a corner point
at the beginning and the end of the drag (**A**). In
the toolbox, there may be a corner tool, which can
originate a corner point with every click, to create
an angular line (**B**).

Each rectangle or square, after ungrouping, consists
of four corner points (**C**). We can then drag any
selected point to distort the shape (**D**) or drag two
selected adjacent points simultaneously to stretch
or compress the shape with a skewing effect (**E**, **F**).

Surprisingly, each ungrouped ellipse or circle also
consists of four corner points (**G**), although the
paths connecting the points are curved. Moving
any of the points can produce noticeable protrusion or indention (**H**).

There are eight corner points on a rounded rectangle or square (**I**), and their shifting can cause considerable distortion of the shape (**J**).

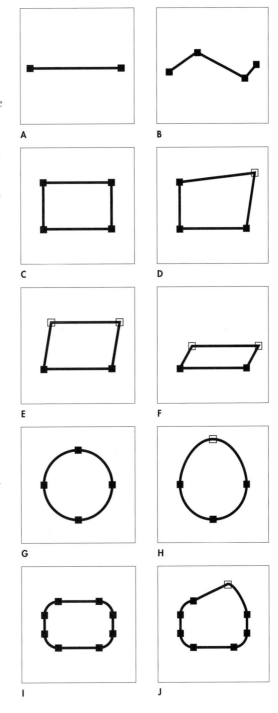

A B C D E F G H I J

POINT HANDLES

Although the ellipse or circle consists of corner points, each of the corner points, upon special selection, appears with a pair of *point handles*, also called "Bézier curve handles" (**A**). Each individual handle of the point can be separately moved to reshape the curvilinearity of an associated path (**B**, **C**).

Sometimes the point handles are fully retracted and invisible. In this case, we can drag a handle out from the point with an arrow tool after depressing the Option key. A straight path (**D**) can become curved with this operation (**E**). If the first dragging has no effect, a second dragging may be necessary to extract another handle.

In an ungrouped rectangle (**F**), an extracted handle can curve an adjacent straight path (**G**). Two extracted handles from the same corner point can curve adjacent paths separately on both sides of the point (**H**). Any handle can be moved back to the point to restraighten the path.

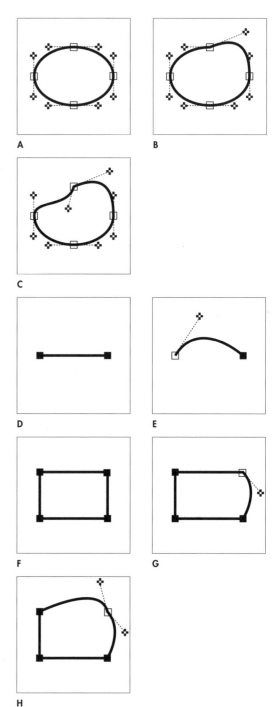

A

B

C

D

E

F

G

H

CURVE POINTS

The second type of point is the *curve point.* A
curve point has a smoothing effect wherever it
occurs. As it effects no protrusion or indention, its
exact location is not easily identifiable if the path
is not selected.

To understand how a curve point works, we can
use a *points* command to substitute a curve point
for a corner point on a selected path. An angular
line (**A**) turns into a curve instantly with the substitution (**B**). The new curve point shows two extracted handles, and each nearby corner point displays
one extracted handle.

On an ungrouped rectangle (**C**), the substitution of
a curve point can turn half of the shape into something like a semicircle, leaving only one of the four
right angles unaffected (**D**). On an ungrouped
ellipse (**E**), curve points at the narrower ends can
make the shape more rounded at those ends (**F**).

Each handle of a curve point may be moved with
the arrow tool in any direction to reshape an adjacent curved path, but the two handles are related,
acting somewhat like a seesaw. If we move one
directly towards or away from its associated curve
point, we may avoid affecting the other handle.

The *curve tool* can be used to create curved paths.
It places a curve point with every click. The curve
of the path, however, is evident probably only
after the third click (**G**). If the last click in the
operation coincides with the first, a closed path
with no angular protrusion or indention results (**H**).

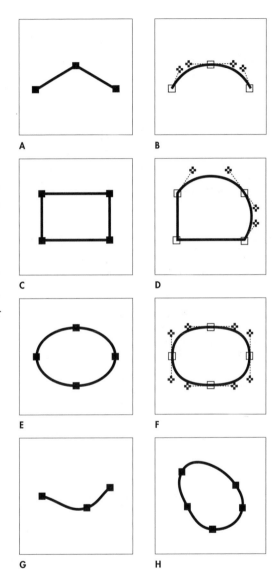

A **B**

C **D**

E **F**

G **H**

CONNECTOR POINTS

64

The third type of point is the *connector point*, which is less common. A connector point enables a straight path to join a curved path while maintaining its original straightness.

Changing one corner point into a connector point on a rectangle produces no immediate effect, as the connector point initially comes with no extending handles (**A**). We can drag a handle out from the connector point to effect the curving of one adjacent path, leaving the other adjacent path straight (**B**). If the first handle effects curving of a wrong segment, we may have to drag the second handle (**C**) and retract the first afterwards.

The handle of the connector point can be moved in only one direction, that is, in the direction of the straight line to which the point connects.

Changing one corner point on an ellipse (**D**) into a connector point produces a protrusion (**E**). Changing two corner points on opposite sides of the shape produces two protrusions (**F**). As there is no straight path on the shape, dragging a handle just distorts it (**G**).

A *connector tool* may be available in the toolbox. Clicking with it initially produces an angular path, similar to that obtained with the corner tool (**H**). Dragging a handle from any of the points will effect a curved segment connected to a straight segment (**I**).

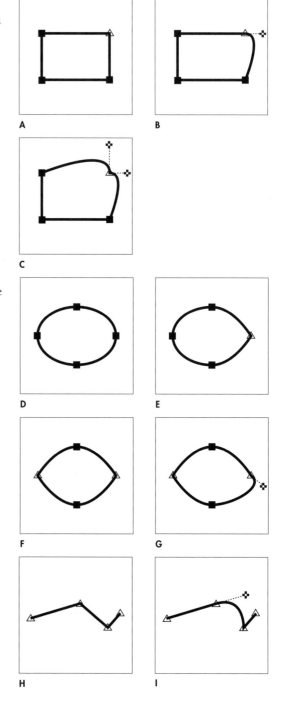

A

B

C

D

E

F

G

H

I

COMBINING POINTS ON A PATH

To produce a path containing more than one type of point, we can use the *freehand tool* or the *pen tool*.

The freehand tool facilitates the drawing of lines in any configuration by freely dragging in any desired direction with smooth or sharp turns (**A**). The resultant path is automatically defined with corner or curve points. If we depress the Option key anytime during dragging, the line becomes straight, but releasing the key returns us to drawing freely formed lines (**B**). We can hold down the Command key and retrace the most recent part of the line to erase that part (**C**).

A pen tool acts like a corner tool to place corner points by mere clicking (**D**). Dragging with the tool cursor, however, places a curve point at the beginning of the drag and a point handle at the end of the drag. Two drags will make a curved path, with the first drag in the ascending direction of the curve, and the second drag in the descending direction, or vice versa (**E**, **F**).

In the middle of dragging with the pen tool to establish a curve, we can hold down the Option key while the mouse button is still depressed, to change the direction of the drag. This results in placing, instead of a curve point, a corner point at the join of two segments, and introduces a protrusion or indention at the join (**G**).

Both the freehand tool and the pen tool can make a closed path if the last point in the operation coincides with the first (**H**).

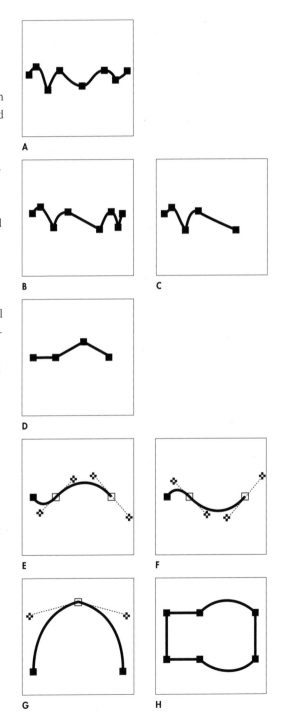

A

B

C

D

E

F

G

H

CREATING PATHS

The freehand tool often produces a path with some irregularity. The pen tool, combining clicking and dragging operations, is for a more experienced user. We can, however, create a path by just clicking with the pen tool, the corner tool, or the connector tool, to establish points that later can be changed to curve points as necessary.

To help with placing points accurately, we can display the rulers, from which we can drag vertical and horizontal guides to construct a nonprinting grid (**A**).

Creating a linear shape similar to the letter "S," we can click four times with the pen or corner tool to obtain a zigzag configuration (**B**), and convert the second and third points into curve points. Subsequently we can move the points and handles to do some reshaping, and assign desirable attributes to the path (**C**).

Alternatively, we can click six times with the connector tool (**D**). With the dragging of handles and possibly the slight shifting of points, an "S" shape with flattened top and bottom paths can result (**E**).

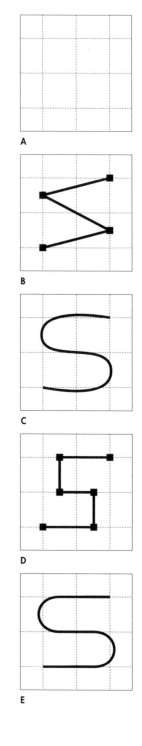

A

B

C

D

E

MODIFYING CLOSED PATHS

Instead of creating a path from scratch, we can originate a basic shape such as a rectangle (**A**), then change it into a different configuration by modifying it in one or more of the following ways:

- Move one or more points after ungrouping the path (**B**, **C**).
- Drag one or two handles from any of the corner points (**D**, **E**).
- Replace any corner point with a curve or connector point (**F**, **G**).
- Add a point of any type by clicking with a tool cursor on the path, and subsequently move the new point and/or move or extract its handles (**H – J**).
- Remove any selected point by striking the Delete key on the keyboard (**K**) and shift any of the remaining points (**L**).
- Regroup the modified path to effect rotation (**M**) or skewing (**N**).

67

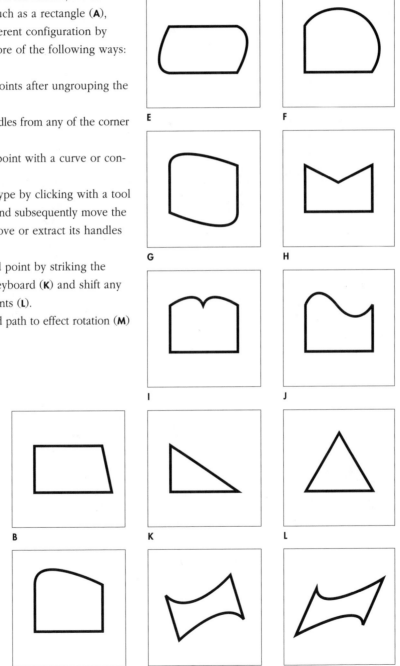

JOINING AND SPLITTING PATHS

A third method of creating a path is by initially creating only a part of the final path. This is most likely an open path, which can be cloned and then rotated or reflected. We can then join the original and the copy after properly positioning them with their end points coinciding.

For instance, guided by a grid we can click six times with the corner tool to obtain half of a star shape (**A**). Subsequently we can clone and reflect the path, and position the copy to the opposite side of the original. The entire shape becomes a closed path when end points of the two halves are joined. We may reach for the *element information* dialog box, using a related command, to ensure or effect closing of the path after joining.

After adjusting positions of the points, we can assign stroke and fill attributes to the path (**B**). For further manipulation, we can substitute some points with curve points and vary the attributes (**C**, **D**).

If desired, we can select the entire star shape and activate the *split element* command to split this closed path into ten separate open paths. The fill may disappear instantly, but now each open path can be variedly stroked (**E**).

Each open path can be split again by engaging a *knife tool* to click somewhere between its two end points. The newly formed open paths can have different stroke attributes (**F**) and possibly a new arrangement (**G**).

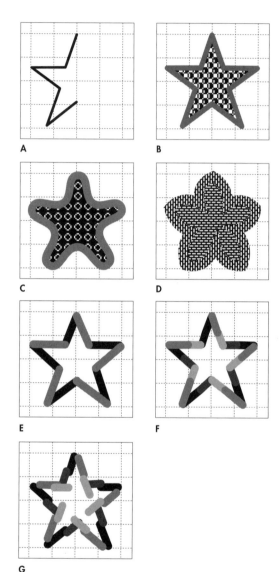

A

B

C

D

E

F

G

SUGGESTED PROBLEMS

Try clicking four times to obtain a closed path (**A**) and developing from this three different heart shapes, one formed from two "C" curves (**B**), one formed from two "S" curves (**C**), and one formed from curved and straight paths featuring connector points (**D**).

Then use one of the heart shapes to make a number of experiments:

- Stroke and fill in numerous ways (**E**, **F**).
- Clone, move, and power-duplicate to obtain a string of three or more heart shapes and join them into a composite shape (**G**).
- Create an elongated ellipse inside the original heart, assign appropriate attributes to each component, and blend them in four or five steps (**H**).
- Split the original path into six or eight open paths and stroke each individually (**I**).

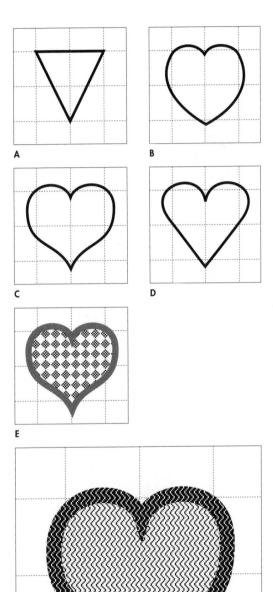

A

B

C

D

E

F

70

G

H

I

6

NNN
NNN
NNN

7 2

The term *type* refers to letters, numbers, punctuation marks, and symbols that can be originated from the keyboard. These are also referred to as *characters*. They offer a wide range of visual possibilities in design and are as important as lines and shapes.

There is a *type tool* in the toolbox for type origination. A special menu head on the menu bar may allow us to access numerous commands providing a choice of options, controls, modifications, transformations, and special effects.

Among all such options, choice of fonts takes precedence over other choices. The computer may come with some popular fonts, and the laser printer may have its resident fonts. Additional fonts can be bought and installed in the computer.

Typography, or typographic design, is a subject unto itself. Our study concentrates on using type as shapes, as individual characters, or as a short title. Using type as body text falls outside the scope of this book.

RANGE OF CHARACTERS

Although there are about sixty keys on a standard keyboard, the total number of characters belonging to just one font could be as many as two hundred.

There are about 47 obtainable with simple clicking on a single key (**A**), and 47 more with the Shift key fully depressed (**B**). Holding down the Option key enables us to access another 47 characters (**C**). Still more characters are available by depressing both the Option and the Shift keys (**D**). In some instances, we may reach special characters with a depressed Control key.

Accent characters require initially clicking the combination of Option-`, Option-e, Option-i, Option-u, or Option-n, and subsequent clicking of the key for the letter (**E**).

A *key caps* desk accessory in the computer's system folder enables us locate most of the characters. Existence of those infrequently used ones should not be overlooked. Characters form words for communication, but may also be used as abstract shapes in a design.

```
`  1 2 3 4 5 6 7 8 9 0 =
q w e r t y u i o p [ ]
 a s d f g h j k l ; '
 z x c v b n m , . / \
```
A

```
~ ! @ # $ % ^ & * ( ) _ +
Q W E R T Y U I O P { }
 A S D F G H J K L : "
 Z X C V B N M < > ? |
```
B

```
¡  ™  £  ¢  ∞  §  ¶  •  ª  º  –  ≠
 œ  Σ  ®  †  ¥  ¨  ø  π  "  '
 å  ß  ƒ  ©  ˙  ∆  °  ¬  …  æ
 Ω  ≈  ç  √  ∫  µ  ≤  ≥  ÷  «
```
C

```
`  ⁄  ¤  ‹ ›  fi fl ‡  °  ·  ,  —  ±
Œ  „  ´  ‰  ˇ  Á  ¨  ^  Ø  ∏  "  '
Å  Í  Î  Ï  ˝  Ó  Ô    Ò  Ú  Æ
   ˛  ¸  Ç  ◊  ₁  ˜  Â  ¯  ˘  ¿  »
```
D

```
Á  á  É  é  Í  í  Ó  ó  Û  ú
À  à  È  è  Ì  ì  Ò  ò  Ù  ù
Â  â  Ê  ê  Î  î  Ô  ô  Û  û
Ä  ä  Ë  ë  Ï  ï  Ö  ö  Ü  ü
     Ã  ã  Õ  õ  Ñ  ñ
```
E

TYPE SIZE

74

Our charts show that characters vary considerably in width and height. Some lowercase letters have *ascenders* as upward-moving strokes (**A** – **B**), some have *descenders* as downward-moving strokes (**C** – **D**), and some have none of these (**E** – **F**). *Type size* is based on measuring the distance from the top of the tallest ascender to the bottom of the longest descender stroke in the entire range.

Disregarding the ascenders and descenders, all letters sit on a *baseline,* and their main body represents the *x-height*, which should not be confused with the type size.

Type size is measured in "points," the same unit of measurement used for the weight of a line, as discussed in chapter 3. The same letter may have a different x-height with font change, and may appear larger or smaller due to type design (**G** – **I**).

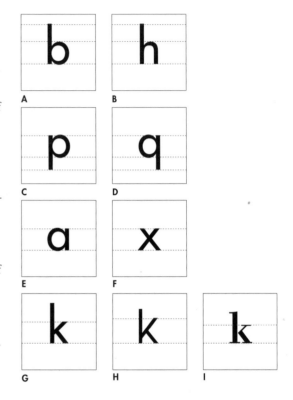

FONTS AND SHAPES

Shapes of characters or letters are determined by the fonts to which they belong. There are two major categories of fonts, the *serifed fonts* and the *sans-serif fonts.*

A serif is a smaller line that joins to or extends a main stroke of a character. It enhances the horizontal progression of words and texts for efficient and legible reading.

A serifed character usually consists of broader vertical strokes in contrast with the thinner horizontal strokes, reflecting the use of a chisel or calligraphic pen, with which the characters were first shaped (**A – C**).

Sans-serif characters have less weight contrast among the strokes (**D – F**). They are usually more geometrically shaped, reflecting a more contemporary spirit, but may be less legible than serifed characters.

VARIATIONS OF A FONT

Changing the line weights and orientations of vertical strokes results in different stylistic variations. Within the same font, usually there are *regular, bold, italic,* and *bold-italic* variations (**G – J**).

Some fonts have separate *light, condensed,* and *extra bold* versions related to one font family, with each version providing separate regular and italicized variations (**K – M**).

Each variation of a font has been specially designed. They are different from stylistic transformations, which the computer can give to all characters, using heavier stroking and skewing effects to attain bold and italicized characters.

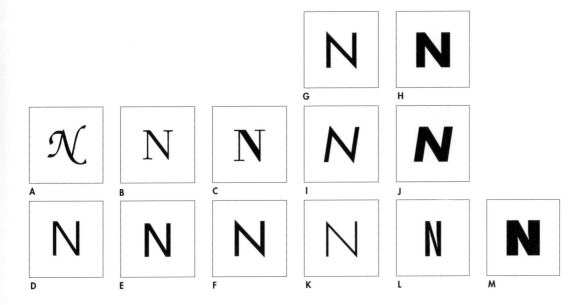

A   B   C   D   E   F   G   H   I   J   K   L   M

SYMBOLS AND DINGBATS

Symbols are shapes that convey meanings. They are used in scientific, engineering, architectural, and other professions, as well as in our daily lives. Dingbats are ornamental types for borders and decorations.

The Symbol font is included in the standard system for any Macintosh computer, and it contains a range of arrows and other shapes that a designer may find useful:

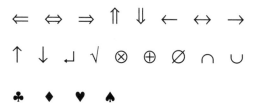

Most laser printers include the Zapf Dingbats among the resident fonts, offering an even greater range of shapes. The following is just a sample selection:

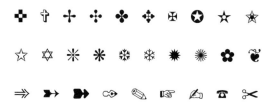

PICTORIAL FONTS

Pictorial fonts consist of mini-pictures, obtainable with the clicking of corresponding keys on the keyboard. The mini-pictures within the font may all relate to one particular theme.

The Cairo font was supplied with earlier Macintosh models. Here is a selection of the mini-pictures provided by this font:

Unlike the Symbol font and the Zapf Dingbats, which are outline fonts for use in any size, the Cairo font is bit-mapped, and may show noticeable jaggedness when enlarged.

DISPLAY FONTS

Display fonts are designed primarily for titles, headlines, and large display texts. The range of characters is sometimes restricted to capital letters, numbers, and common punctuation marks. In addition, display fonts are frequently composed of extremely bold strokes or finely delineated elements of considerable complexity, and can have clarity only above a particular type size.

Such fonts may have a decorative feeling or show expressive qualities to meet with specialized requirements in design and communication.

Here are some letters of the Slipstream font, from Letraset's Fontek collection, conveying a sense of movement and velocity:

The above characters were set in a 72-point size so that all the fine linear details can be seen clearly. In any smaller point size, much of the detail will be lost.

STYLISTIC TRANSFORMATIONS

The computer can effect stylistic transformations to characters of all fonts. The transformations are italic (oblique), bold (heavy), outline, and shadow, all based on the original plain version. The different transformations may be combined. The following is a demonstration of such transformations, using an arrow shape from Zapf Dingbats to obtain a number of variations:

- plain
- italic
- bold
- outline
- shadow
- italic + outline
- italic + shadow
- italic + outline + shadow
- outline + shadow

MANIPULATING CHARACTERS

In a drawing program, any individual character or string of characters first originated on screen is contained in a nonprinting text box with one corner handle at each of the four corners, and probably also one side handle along each of the four edges, totalling eight handles altogether (**A**).

Using the arrow key, we can drag one of its left- or right-side handles horizontally to increase or decrease the space between characters (**B**, **C**).

To change the size and/or proportion of characters, we can drag with the scaling tool, but we can also use the arrow tool as we hold down the Option key in advance (**D** – **F**).

We can rotate, reflect, and skew the characters with the respective tools (**G** – **I**). Such manipulations can be effected in a sequence (**J** – **N**).

E   F

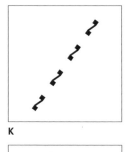

G   H

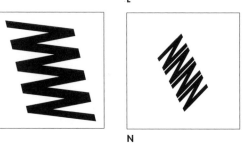

I   J

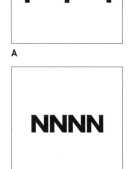

A   B

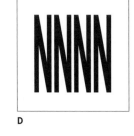

K   L

C   D

M   N

STROKING AND FILLING CHARACTERS

All characters first appearing on screen have a solid black fill but no strokes (**A**). The black fill can be replaced with a shade of gray or white by choosing an option in the color palette (**B**).

The characters can be stroked and filled in any of the gray shades as well as white. There may be an *effect* command providing different options for this purpose (**C**, **D**).

Stroking the characters with a heavy line weight can link them together in one unusual shape (**E**).

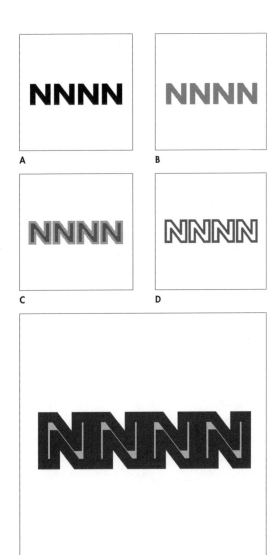

SPECIAL EFFECTS

80

We can obtain special effects, such as *inline* and *zoom text* transformations, from the same command used for stroking and filling.

Inline transformation adds concentric line layers to the characters, with specified line weight, shades, and number of iterated lines (**A**, **B**).

Zoom text transformation creates a three-dimensional effect. The characters can be zoomed to any direction with horizontal and/or vertical offset and with increase or decrease of size. Positive figures in units of points can offset characters to the right and up, whereas negative figures can offset them to the left and down.

Our demonstrations here show characters zoomed 100 percent, with offset of 20 points horizontal and 20 points vertical (**C**), 20 points horizontal and -20 points vertical (**D**), -20 points horizontal and 20 points vertical (**E**), -20 points horizontal and -20 points vertical (**F**), and -20 points horizontal and 0 point vertical (**G**). Two further examples show the same characters zoomed 75 percent and 200 percent with offset of 0 point horizontal and -20 points vertical (**H**, **I**).

Each the above includes a copy of the original in appropriate attributes, placed directly in front to enhance legibility of the characters.

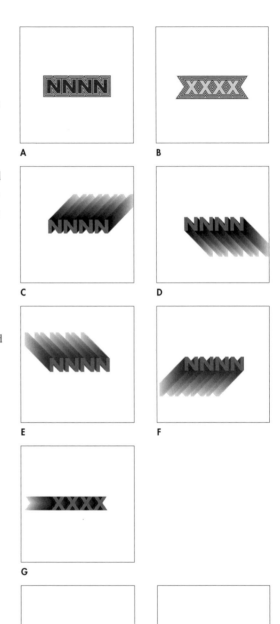

A

B

C

D

E

F

G

H

I

JOINING CHARACTERS TO PATHS

We can join a line of characters to a straight open path, a curved open path, a circle, or an ellipse, with the *join elements* command, which has options relating to the orientation of the characters.

All angled characters will result if a diagonally placed line of characters joins to a horizontal straight path (**A**). Characters joined to an ellipse can rotate along the path, remain vertical, or skew vertically (**B – D**). Two lines of characters, separated by hitting the Return or Enter key, can wrap around the ellipse without any line turning upside down (**E**).

We can join characters to a curved open path and have them rotating around the path, remaining vertical, being skewed vertically, or being skewed horizontally (**F – I**).

The path usually disappears after the joining operation, but it is visible in the keyline mode. We can always reshape the path by dragging any point or point handle to change the arrangement of characters (**J**).

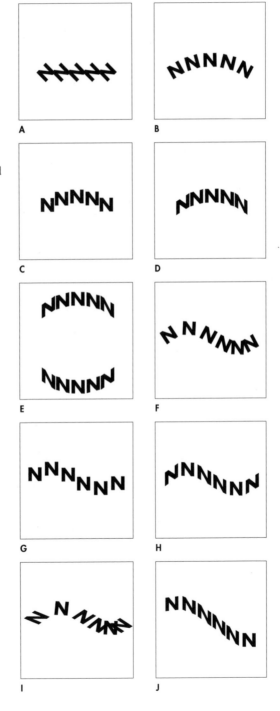

A

B

C

D

E

F

G

H

I

J

CONVERSION TO PATHS

8 2

Instead of using the effect command to accomplish stroking and filling, we can convert the characters into editable paths with the *convert to paths* command. After conversion, the characters become one composite shape, bounded with four object handles at the corners.

We can now give the characters a gradient or radial fill, which will extend from one end to another (**A**, **B**). We can also stroke and fill the characters with patterns (**C**, **D**).

All the characters are fully joined, although they look separated. To move individual characters, we have to use the *split element* command. After splitting, each character becomes an individual shape. Any gradient fill will not extend from one character to the next (**E**).

The advantages of splitting are numerous. We can move each character to any position (**F**). If the characters are closely overlapping, we can stroke them with white (**G**) or assign each different attributes (**H**). We can vary the size and proportion of each character, and can effect rotation, reflection, or skewing if desired (**I**).

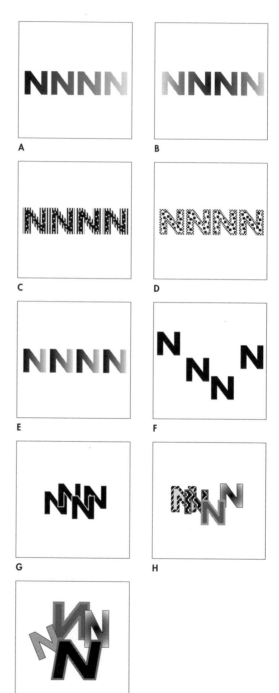

A

B

C

D

E

F

G

H

I

EXPRESSING MEANING

The meaning of a word can be enhanced in a visual way. We can attain special expression with changes of font, size, attributes, or other aspects of the individual characters. Conversion to paths may facilitate such changes. Here are some examples:

- Mix fonts in the word "TYPE" (**A**).
- Substitute a dingbat in the word "LOVE" (**B**).
- Use arrow shapes to replace the two Is in the word "DIRECTION" (**C**).
- Reflect a character in the word "MIRROR" (**D**).
- Change scale and proportion in the word "ASCENT" (**E**).
- Rotate a character in the word "FALL" (**F**).
- Skew some characters in the word "CONFLICT" (**G**).
- Introduce different attributes in the word "VARIETY" (**H**).

D

E

F

A

B

G

C

H

SUGGESTED PROBLEMS

8 4   Try originating the word "STRETCH" to obtain a
number of copies ready for the following experiments:

- Elongate, skew, and rotate some of the copies
  in different way; fill them with different gray
  shades; and arrange them inside a large, outlined square (**A**).
- Fill the large square in black or dark gray;
  change some of the copies to white; further
  skew and rotate them in a new arrangement.
  Rescale and reflect if necessary (**B**).
- Create seven small ellipses. Convert one copy
  of the word into paths and split it into separate characters. Group each character with one
  ellipse, which may be filled, rotated, and
  skewed (**C**).
- Use two or more skewed copies and apply
  zoom text transformations. Subsequently
  arrange them, and rotate them if necessary,
  inside a large, filled or unfilled square (**D**).

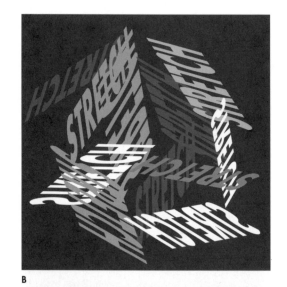

B

C

A

D

8 6

Although a draw program can meet most of our visual needs, there are certain effects that can be achieved or better achieved only with a paint program.

With a paint program, we need to take a different approach than we would with a draw program. Shapes are no longer objects that can be picked up and moved around at any time. They are images as opaque marks, as transparent stains or scattered dots, and as spreading textures that are sometimes vaguely defined.

Compared with what we can get from a draw program, results produced by a paint program may be of a much lower resolution, with shapes exhibiting some jaggedness along curved and slanting edges. Most operations in a paint program are irreversible, except for the simple undoing of the latest operations, and generally there is less control for precise work.

For a sense of directness and spontaneity, for richness of texture, for intentional imperfection, and for a close simulation of hand-sketched or hand-painted results, a paint program might be the right choice. Most paint programs can handle color and grayscale with considerable refinement, and painted images can always be transferred to a draw program for further development.

WORKING WITH TYPE

Any paint program provides a type tool similar to the type tool included in draw programs. Characters obtained in a paint program can be collectively or individually selected with a *marquee tool* or a *lasso tool.* The marquee tool is for drawing a rectangle that selects all it covers, including the blank space. The lasso tool is for making a loop that tightens up to surround any positive shape it encompasses. Selection by lassoing is often preferable, since no unwanted blank space outside the character will be included. Each character or the entire line of characters may be moved after selection.

All characters are initially in solid black (**A**), but can be filled individually. After choosing a pattern, we use the *fill tool* to click on each character to apply an appropriate fill (**B**). We can have different patterns for different characters (**C**).

Some grayscale paint programs may allow us to use a gradient fill of any direction (**D**, **E**), a radial fill with circular (**F**) or rectangular transitions (**G**), or a "peaked" gradient fill with ridge-like highlights (**H**). Gradient fills can be customized with light-dark iteration (**I**). Radial fills can have off-positioned centers (**J**).

A

B

C

D

E

F

G

H

I

J

TRANSFORMATIONS AND DISTORTIONS

88

The characters can be transformed or distorted individually or as a line of text, not with tools but with specific commands. We should use solid black characters before any transformation or distortion, as bit-mapped patterns always change with the shape and may get unpleasantly uneven after transformation or distortion.

Once a respective command is activated, the selected character or characters will be contained in a frame with four handles (**A**), each of which can be moved. With a *scaling* command, pushing or pulling a handle effects enlargement or reduction of size, with or without stretching or compressing (**B** – **D**).

After scaling, we can reach for the *skewing* command to slant the character or characters in any direction (**E**, **F**), and we can use the *rotating* command for free rotation (**G**). There is also a command for horizontal or vertical flipping of any selected image (**H**, **I**).

A *perspective distortion* command may be available, for changing the selected image so that it is wider at one side or end and narrower at the other side or end (**J**, **K**). A *free distortion* command can deform the image considerably (**L**, **M**).

After transformation or distortion, saw-tooth jaggedness can become intolerably prominent along some edges. Filling with a pattern or gradient of any kind usually can make the jaggedness less noticeable (**N** – **P**).

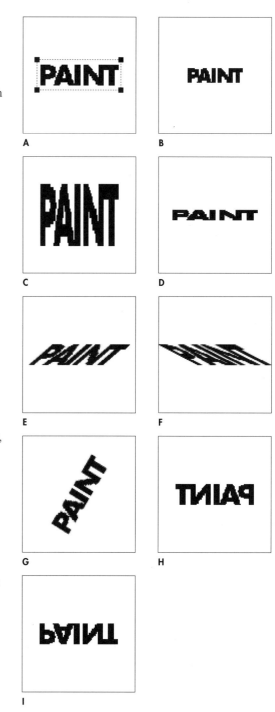

A

B

C

D

E

F

G

H

I

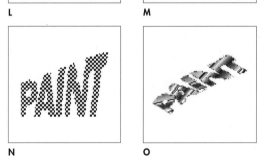

J K

L M

N O

P

EDITING BIT-MAPPED IMAGES

Transformed or distorted images may require subsequent editing. A magnified view next to the normal view of any spot can be obtained by clicking with a *magnifying tool.* All affected pixels will appear in the form of connected or disconnected square dots. Using the normal view as a reference, we can engage the *pencil tool* to perform pixel editing by clicking on a blank spot to add a dot, or on an existing dot to remove it.

Deletion of large areas may require the *eraser tool.* For utmost flexibility, there is the *brush tool,* which can use black-and-white paint from a color palette, and a variety of tip sizes and shapes, to do broad and fine editing work.

For complete removal of all jaggedness, we may need a combined paint/draw program, such as Aldus SuperPaint, to edit bit-mapped images as "SuperBits." This term is used in Aldus SuperPaint to refer to the much finer bits replacing the original coarse bits as the image is transferred from the paint layer to the draw layer. The SuperBits can be magnified and edited with all paint tools.

Our examples show a distorted painted image before and after editing as SuperBits (**Q**, **R**). This image is now ready for higher-resolution printing.

89

Q

R

SOFTENING THE IMAGE

90

Another way of removing the jaggedness of a painted image is by softening its edges. Some paint programs may provide an *antialiasing* command to effect this automatically when we are working in grayscale. Antialiasing is the creation of transitional shades along an edge to bridge adjacent shades, or a shade and the white of the screen. We can get flat shapes as well as type with antialiased edges (**A**, **B**), which can be transformed or distorted with less obvious jaggedness (**C**, **D**).

Antialiasing can be accomplished manually with a *smudge tool.* This comes with variable tip sizes, and can blend pixels of different shades. We can use a fine tip to go over the entire edge of the image in a magnified view. The resultant image may show slight irregularity in the softening (**E**). The smudge tool with a broad tip can blur an image considerably (**F**).

There may be an *airbrush tool* for simulating a fine mist of paint in black, white, or any gray shade. We can use it to soften edges, but its main purpose is for lightening or darkening an area, showing passing trails of the tool (**G**). This tool can sprinkle irregularly shaped larger drops of paint if desired (**H**).

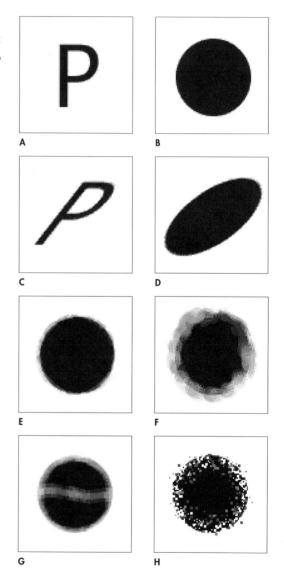

A   B
C   D
E   F
G   H

BRUSH EFFECTS

The brush tool has far more uses than just image editing. In fact, it is often considered the main tool in a paint program. Its tip comes in a range of sizes and shapes, which can also be specially modified (**A – D**). We use the brush to create freely formed shapes in black, any shade of gray, or any available or customized pattern or texture (**E – H**).

There are several transfer modes in a palette that enable us to *paint* with the brush tool on the blank screen or on top of other images. The brush mark can cover any underlying image and background in the *opaque* mode (**I**). In the *translucent* mode, any darker part of the underlying image will show through (**J**). The *transparent* mode lightens the brush shade in a specified percentage and allows any underlying image to be seen clearly (**K**). In the *invert* mode, what the brush mark overlaps will change to the white of the screen or to an entirely different shade (**L**). There is also the *paint-on-darker* mode, with which the brush mark affects only the darker pixels of the image and not the white of the background (**M**).

Brush marks can have gradient fills in all or most of the above transfer modes (**N – Q**). We can drag any isolated brush mark after lassoing or marqueeing it. In marqueeing, we can choose the *transparent background* option, an additional option in the transfer modes palette, so that any marqueed background will not be obtrusive. Holding down the Option key as we drag any lassoed or marqueed mark, we can drag a copy of the mark and leave the original where it is (**R**). Individual copies can be changed in shade or pattern with the fill tool before they are moved to overlap one another in a composition (**S**, **T**).

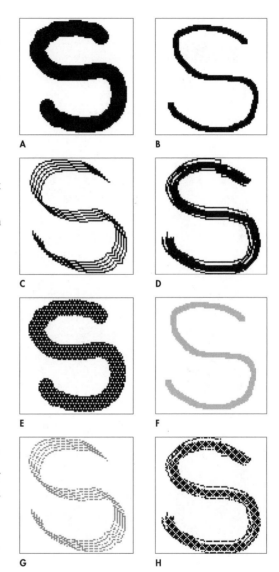

A

B

C

D

E

F

G

H

92

I

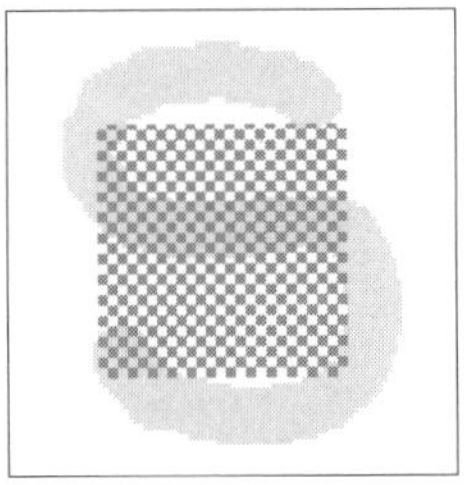

J

R

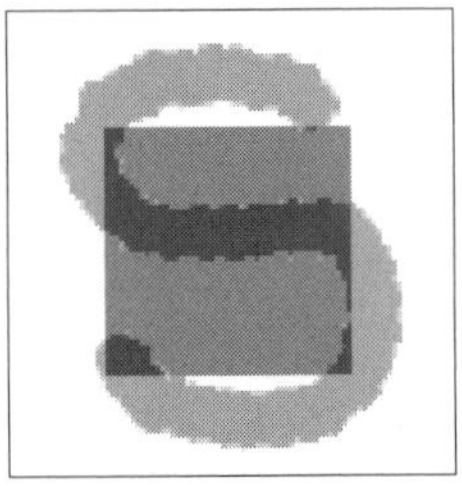

K

L

S

M

N

O

P

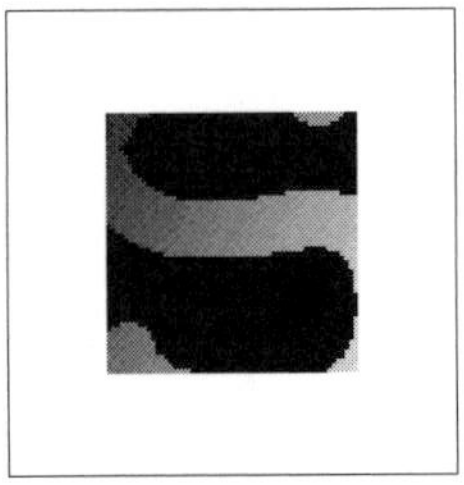

T

Q

BRUSH SYMMETRY

Some programs facilitate the use of the brush tool for instantly creating a symmetrical or radiating shape with kaleidoscopic effects. A dialog box associated with the *brush symmetry* command may be available for specifying the number of repeats and their arrangements.

A brush stroke can be mirrored twice, four times, or eight times, along a vertical, horizontal, left-inclined diagonal or right-inclined diagonal axis (**A** – **D**). It can also be radially repeated two or more times in a full revolution (**E** – **H**).

Brush symmetry can be effected with different transfer modes (**I** – **K**), and can be used with patterns and gradients on a white, black, shaded, or gradient background (**L** – **O**).

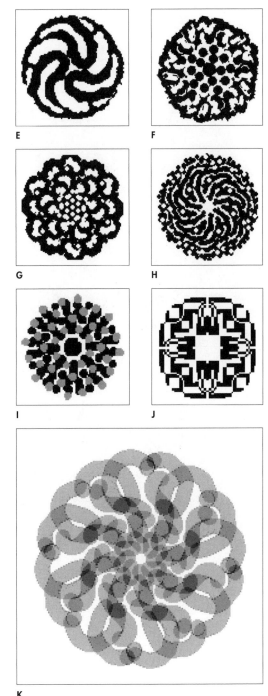

E

F

G

H

I

J

A

B

C

D

K

94

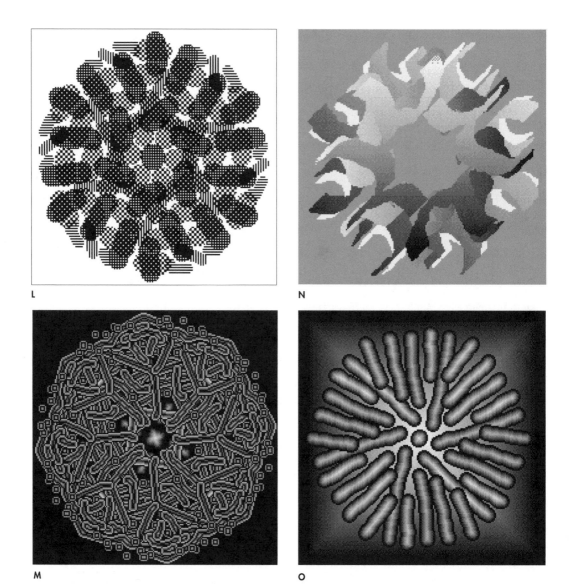

L

N

M

O

WORKING WITH SHAPE TOOLS

All paint programs have a few shape tools, typically the rectangle tool, the ellipse tool, and the rounded rectangular tool, which are very similar to their counterparts in a draw program. There may be also a *polygon tool* for creating rectilinear shapes.

We can specify line weight for the frame of the shape, as well as pattern or shade separately for the frame and its enclosed space, similar to assigning stroke and fill attributes in a draw program (**A**, **B**). All gradient effects can be applied to either the frame or the enclosed space (**C** – **F**).

We can frame any image by dragging a shape tool over it without covering the image (**G**, **H**), or have a veil of pattern spreading above it, with or without the frame (**I**, **J**). If the paint-on-darker mode is in effect, with no line weight for the frame, we can drag a shape tool to cover an underlying image with a pattern without affecting the background (**K**), and can apply different patterns to different parts of the image in a sequence of operations (**L**).

C

D

E

F

G

H

I

J

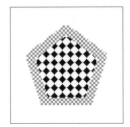

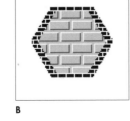

A

B

K

L

MASKING THE IMAGE

96

After one part of an image is marqueed or lassoed, we can use a *masking* command to turn that part or the surrounding area into a mask. Subsequently we can use the brush tool, the airbrush tool, or any other tool to add marks or texture along the edges of the mask. Whatever is underneath the mask remains unaffected (**A**, **B**). There are commands for temporary removal or permanent deletion of the mask.

Some paint programs provide a range of marquee tools in circular, polygonal, and other shapes (**C** – **E**), and may allow the addition and subtraction of shapes to an existing mask (**F**, **G**).

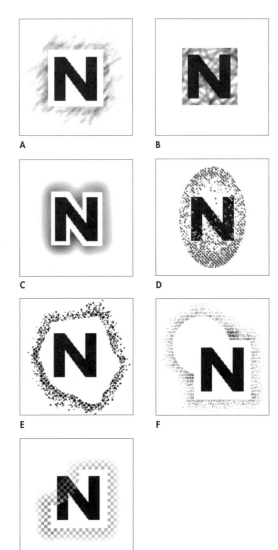

A   B

C   D

E   F

G

BREAKING UP THE IMAGE

It is relatively easy to break up a painted image with the lasso or marquee tool. We can use the lasso tool to draw an enclosed shape on top of the image and drag the lassoed area away from it (**A**). The marquee tool marks off a rectangular area on the image for dragging apart, but any background area included in the marqueed area will also be dragged as a white shape unless a transparent background option is chosen among the transfer modes (**B**, **C**). The image can be broken up into specially shaped parts if shaped marquee tools are available (**D – F**).

Each part of a broken-up image may be individually filled if desired (**G**). A transparent image may be broken up with overlapping parts that can be seen through (**H**, **I**).

We can also break up an image by using the pencil tool to delete pixels, suggesting cracks and dents, and move some separated parts with the lasso or marquee tool if necessary (**J**).

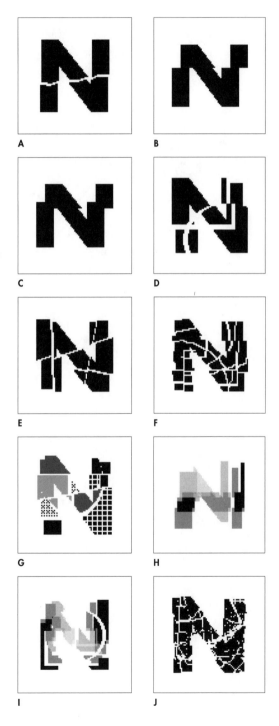

A

B

C

D

E

F

G

H

I

J

TRACING PAINTED IMAGES

A painted image that is not texturized and has definable edges can be traced within a combined paint/draw program. After tracing, the image becomes a drawn object composed of points and paths.

We can transfer the painted image to a separate draw program by copying it to the clipboard or the scrapbook, and subsequently pasting it to a document window of the draw program.

If the painted image is complex, automatic tracing does not always lead to satisfactory results. The resultant path may contain more points than necessary. Certain details of the original image may be distorted and require subsequent editing.

On the draw layer of a combined program or in a draw program, we can use any appropriate tool to perform manual tracing, probably with the image scaled in a convenient large size. In this way, we can also make changes as we trace.

After tracing, the painted image (**A**) may be discarded, for the newly created shape as a closed path can be edited, stroked, filled, resized, or transformed (**B – E**). This new shape is completely free of all jaggedness.

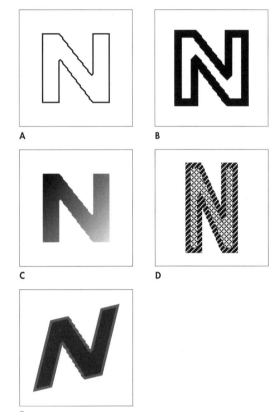

A

B

C

D

E

SUGGESTED PROBLEMS

Try originating the word "TYPE" in solid black with the type tool and move the characters closely to touch or overlap one another (**A**). Subsequently try proceeding with the following steps:

- Copy the image to the clipboard. Make a few copies for immediate use.
- Use two copies, one right way up and one rotated 180 degrees to form a composition, and fill each with a different pattern, shade, or gradient (**B**).
- Use four copies to form a rectangular arrangement. Use the ellipse tool to apply an area of pattern at the center of the arrangement, with the paint-on-darker transfer mode in effect, and use the brush tool to add freely more patterned areas (**C**).

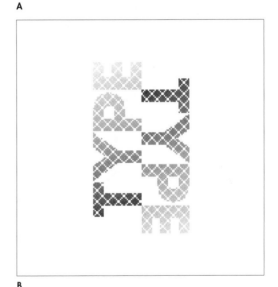

A

B

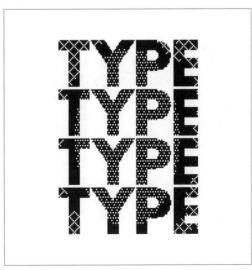

C

100

- Use four copies, progressively rotated 90 degrees, to form a square-shape enclosure. Spray different shades of gray paint, with a chosen pattern, on the characters with the airbrush tool. Clean up the enclosed area with the eraser tool, or mask that area before spraying (**D**).

- Stretch and skew a copy and fill it with a transparent gray shade. Obtain two or more copies from this and arrange them to show their transparent effect with overlapping (**E**).

- Arrange four copies, with two flipped vertically, to form a rectangular shape. Use a circular marquee tool to mark off a part at the center, rotate that part 5 to 15 degrees, and move it slightly. Then break up the image further with marqueeing or lassoing. Use the pencil tool to introduce some irregularities and fill some disintegrated parts with different patterns (**F**).

E

D

F

8

102

Any black-and-white line art that has been hand-drawn, photocopied, or printed, and any grayscale or color image that has been hand-painted, printed, or photographed, can be brought to the computer for use as is or for further development. This requires a hand-held or flat-bed scanner, which converts the artwork into a scanned image that can be easily edited.

The scanned image is very similar to a painted image, as it is composed of tiny square pixels that can be seen clearly upon magnification. It does not consist of points and paths, even if it shows only solid outlines.

A scanner usually comes with its own software program for initial editing of the scanned image. For extensive editing and modifications, we can transfer the image to a color or grayscale paint program. More demanding work may require a specialized image-editing program, such as Adobe PhotoShop, for which a range of transformation filters is also available.

The scanned image can be imported to a draw program to work with other shapes. The image can be used as it is, but can also be rescaled, stretched, rotated, reflected, or skewed. It can serve as a template for automatic or manual tracing.

THE SCANNING PROCESS

Scanning often covers a rectangular plane. What is
scanned includes not just the image, but also its
background on the sheet of paper containing the
image "seen" by the scanner. In a black-and-white
scan, the white background of the image is usually
dropped out completely (**A**), but a grayscale image
often comes with the background (**B**).

There may be separate settings for black-and-white
and grayscale images, and for different resolutions.
After scanning, brightness and contrast are always
adjustable with a gray-map editor in the scanning
program. The image can then be saved in any of
the following formats for subsequent use with
other programs:

- PAINT. The image is stored as a black-and-
  white bit-mapped file with a low, 72-dpi resolution. It can get gummed up when reduced,
  or show serrated edges when enlarged.
- TIFF (Tagged Image File Format). The image is
  stored as a high-resolution bit-mapped file
  with grayscale and color information. A TIFF
  image can be enlarged or reduced with much
  greater flexibility than the PAINT image. It
  occupies considerable memory but may be
  compressed for storage.
- PICT. The image is bit-mapped and stored as
  an object, but individual pixels are usually not
  editable. All draw programs and the clipboard
  support this format.
- EPS (Encapsulated PostScript). The image is
  displayed on screen as a PICT image, but
  accompanied with the PostScript language for
  working with high-resolution printers.

A

B

103

HAND-DRAWN IMAGES

104

We can sketch our design ideas or trace any existing image with pencil or marker on paper, and scan the results for reworking in a paint program.

The hand-drawn image may have just a black outline with or without antialiased edges (**A**). We can broaden the line with the brush tool if necessary (**B**). Any black line that is not too thin can be filled with a shade, a pattern, or even a gradient (**C**).

We can also fill any enclosed plane (**D**, **E**) and the background (**F**, **G**).

B

A

C

D

F

E

G

PRINTED IMAGES

106

Any existing image printed in solid black ink can be scanned and transferred to a paint program for considerable modification.

It may consists of lines and planes that are not all connected (**A**). We can fill each of these with the fill tool (**B**), or overpaint them separately with the brush tool in the paint-on-darker mode to get a variety of patterns on the same image (**C**).

The image can be duplicated, scaled, stretched, and rotated. Superimposing duplicated images in the transparent mode, we can have a pictorial effect of illusory depth (**D**). Transparent and opaque modes can be combined on a filled background with images in different shades (**E**).

We can make the image white by dragging over it with the rectangle tool in the *invert* mode with a chosen pattern. Subsequently we can place a duplicate of the original image in black on top and sprinkle some light gray dots, to create the effect of a snowing scene (**F**).

The image can stand out in relief with a black shadow behind. We can give the image and the background separate gradient fills (**G**).

The image can be converted into outlines, either within a combined paint/draw program or in a draw program (**H**).

A

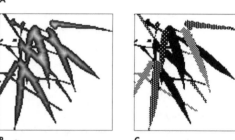

B   C

D

E

G

F

H

PHOTOGRAPHIC IMAGES

108

Photographic images usually contain continuous tones and should be scanned in grayscale. If the photograph is an isolated object, after scanning we can remove the background with the eraser tool in the scanning program (**A**).

The image may require some adjustment in brightness and contrast (**B**). We can use the gray-map editor for this purpose, but we can use it also to manipulate the distribution of grays, with reduction of gray levels to three or four to attain the effect of *posterization* (**C**), or with arbitrary conversion of parts of the darker areas into white or light gray to obtain numerous interesting versions of the same image (**D – F**).

A grayscale image is usually printed in a fine regular pattern of halftone dots. We can, however, have it *dithered* as bit-mapped patterns, several options for which are available. The *Bayer* pattern has an orderly arrangements of dots in horizontal rows and vertical columns (**G**). The *error diffusion* pattern has the dots somewhat freely distributed (**H**). The *random* pattern shows dots more in a woven-like arrangement (**I**). Resolution and density of the patterns are adjustable.

A

B

C

D

E

F

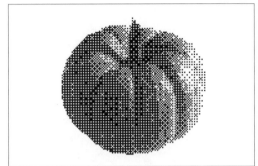

G

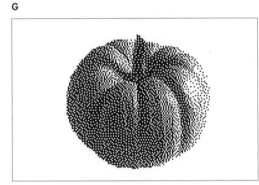

H

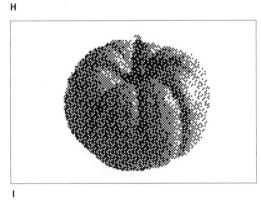

I

OVERPAINTING THE IMAGE

110

Through overpainting, the scanned photographic image can simulate a hand-painted image. This should be done in a paint program where the full range of paint tools are available.

We can cover the entire image with a pattern, using the rectangle tool in the paint-on-darker mode (**A**). This does not change its photographic characteristics, but subsequently we can use the brush tool to add patterned strokes (**B**).

The entire image can be covered with broad and thin strokes in gradients (**C**), with strokes combined with sprayed dots in various sizes and shades, or with softening smudges (**D**), to the extent that the original photographic image is hardly discernible.

Some paint programs even facilitate reinterpretation of the image as a pointillistic painting (**E**) or a pencil drawing (**F**).

A

B

C

E

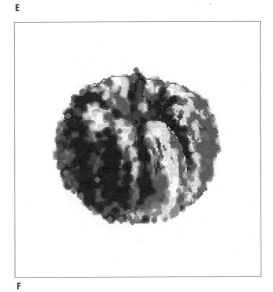

D

F

TRACING THE IMAGE

112

We can import the scanned photographic image as a template for tracing in a draw program. Tracing must be done manually, as the light and dark patterns of the image do not have clear area divisions for automatic tracing.

To do manual tracing, we can use the freehand tool for a complex shape, or use one of the point tools for graceful curves and straight lines. The resultant drawing, initially in a fine line (**A**), can be restroked in any desired line weight (**B**), shade, or pattern (**C**).

This line drawing cannot be filled, as it comprises mainly open paths. At this stage, we can stroke it in solid black with an appropriate line weight (**D**), and use the *tracing tool* to perform automatic tracing along the two edges of the lines.

After tracing, we can remove the original line drawing to discover the shape rendered in double lines, which are all closed paths (**E**). Each area now can be filled. The general surrounding outline of the shape can be retained (**F**) or removed (**G**). We can stroke all the outlines, fill the background as desired (**H – J**), and add smaller areas to be filled as details (**K**).

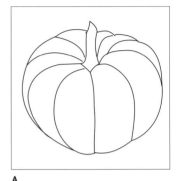

A

B

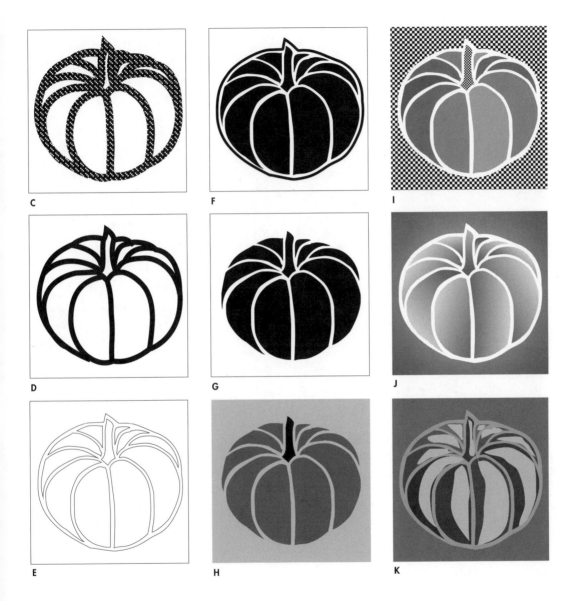

C

F

I

D

G

J

E

H

K

TRANSFORMING THE IMAGE

In a draw program, the scanned photograph may be imported as a strictly black-and-white image, which can be subsequently attributed any gray shade (**A**). The image can be duplicated, rescaled, rotated, reflected, or transformed, and it can be placed on a filled background (**B**, **C**).

We can trace and convert it into an outlined image (**D**), which can be stroked and filled (**E**), as well as duplicated, rescaled, rotated, reflected, or transformed (**F**). Two or more of such images may be joined as a group to show the effect of interpenetration (**G**).

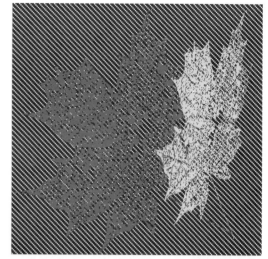

B

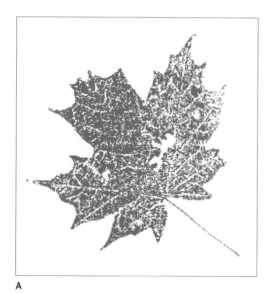

A

C

D

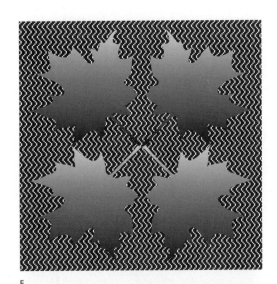

F

E

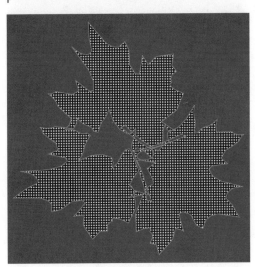

G

USING SPECIAL FILTERS

The transformation of scanned images can be accomplished automatically with special filters provided in image-editing programs. Most filters are just for lightening or darkening selected areas, hardening or softening edges, adding speckles, or smoothing out textures.

Filters can be compared to special-purpose lenses for cameras, though there are special filters for usual effects and distortions that are probably more for the designer than for the photo-retoucher. Each special filter transforms images in a particular way. How any filter will work with a selected image is not always predictable. A filter for spherical distortion could render a natural image (**A**) nearly unrecognizable (**B**).

We can use a filter to blur an image. In an extreme case, the image suggests a faint shade and quick motion (**C**). Conversely, we can use a filter to increase the visibility of the image by giving it a heavy border (**D**).

An appropriate filter can enable us to convert an image into a realistic bas-relief (**E**) or mosaic work (**F**), to enclose it within its own multiple images (**G**), or to create effects accomplishable with pen and ink (**H**), woodcut (**I**), watercolor (**J**), or dry brush and paint (**K**).

A

B

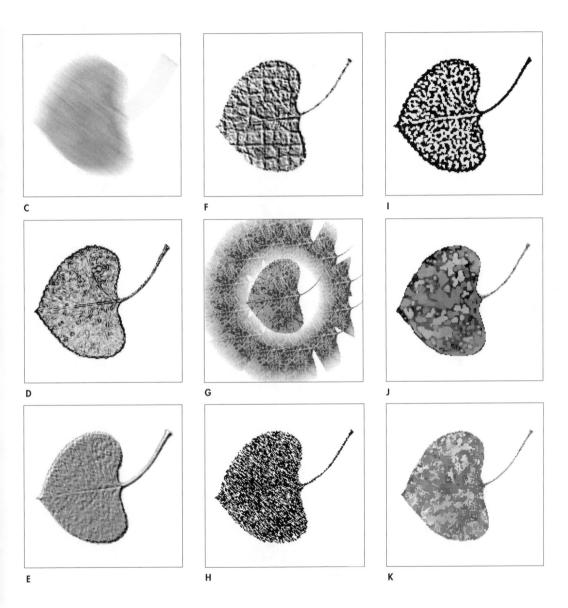

C

F

I

D

G

J

E

H

K

SUGGESTED PROBLEMS

118

Try modifying a scanned black-and-white image created with brush and ink in a paint program:

- Use the brush in a paint-on-darker mode and apply patterns to different areas (**A**).
- Select a pattern and spray unevenly with the airbrush tool (**B**).
- Stretch and obtain a reflection of the image, fill the original, its reflection and the background with different gradients (**C**).
- Duplicate the image two or more times and arrange the results in transparent and opaque modes on a filled ground already containing a negative of the image (**D**).
- Transfer the image to a draw program and trace its outline (**E**).
- Stroke the traced image with a heavy line weight in a pattern, and fill the image and the background with different patterns (**F**).

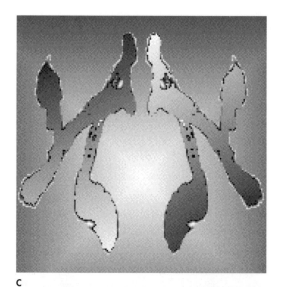

C

D

A

B

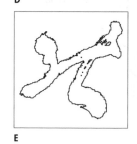

E

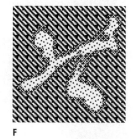

F

120

A *shape* is a fairly distinctive visual entity. It occupies a definite amount of space and has attributes that render it visible. It consists of elements, which are the points and paths.

Points establish either open or closed paths. Paths define the overall visual appearance or configuration of the shape, its vertices, edges, surfaces, angles, and dimensions.

An *aggregate* is formed when a number of shapes interacting with one another are seen as a group. Shapes then become components or *units* when they are contituents of the aggregate.

One or more shapes or aggregates can constitute a composition. A composition is the total visual effect, including all that is perceived as occupied and unoccupied space on a flat surface defined with a border.

DEFINITION OF A SHAPE

With an idea for a shape in mind, we can start with
a straight line, a curve, a rectangle, an ellipse, a
letter, a dingbat, or a painted or scanned image,
and seek various possible changes that would lead
to the realization and refinement of that idea.

Changes can be made through the addition, deletion, and substitution of points, the shifting of
positions, and probably also the dragging of handles. Any resultant shape can then be transformed
and assigned desired attributes.

In a narrow sense, we could define a shape as a
visible object comprising one single open or closed
path. If we use letter forms as examples, we can
regard C, I, J, L, M, N, S, U, V, W, and Z as single
open paths, and D and O as closed paths. All other
letters would fail to meet the definition.

In a broader sense, we could define a shape as
containing all visually connected elements and
having no more than one enclosure of space. This
means that a shape can include as many open
paths as desirable (**A**) but only one closed path (**B**).
Now all other letters can qualify as shapes, with
the probable exception of the letter B.

Open paths in a shape can have as few as two
points (**C**, **D**), or can be more complicated and have
many sharp turns, loops, and knots with numerous
points (**E** – **G**). A closed path can also have as few
as two points (**H**, **I**), and can show sharp turns,
loops, and knots (**J** – **L**).

LINEAR SHAPES

1 2 2

Shapes comprising all open paths are linear shapes, which can be stroked but not filled.

We can bring an end point of one open path to touch an end point of another open path. If we join the two paths, they will have identical attributes (**A**, **B**). If we leave them unjoined, we can assign them different attributes (**C**, **D**).

One open path can touch the middle part of another open path (**E**, **F**). It can also cross or over-lap the other (**G**, **H**). In both cases, the paths can-not be joined, but may be grouped.

An open path can make a loop to enclose space (**I**). Two or more open paths can also enclose space (**J**). Space enclosed in such ways cannot be filled.

Two angular open paths of different shades, or patterns overlapping one another and enclosing space, cannot form an interlocking shape, as one path always remains in front of the other (**K**). One path must be split at a join to become two separate new paths, so that we can send one of these to the back to interlock with the other path (**L**).

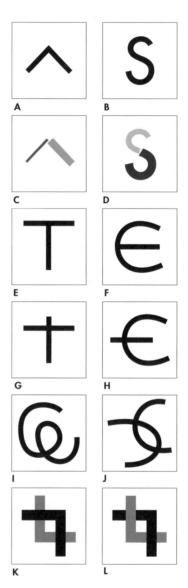

A   B

C   D

E   F

G   H

I   J

K   L

PLANAR SHAPES

Linear shapes are easy to construct, but they have visual limitations. For instance, the caps remain squared or round when a line is skewed (**A** – **C**). Round or beveled joins are automatic and may not have the right configurations.

We can, however, easily trace the edges of a linear shape (**D**) with the tracing tool to obtain a closed path (**E**). This closed path can now be reshaped or transformed (**F**), filled but not stroked (**G**), stroked but not filled (**H**), or both stroked and filled (**I**).

We can convert any chosen character into a planar shape containing a closed path (**J**) and develop entirely new shapes with stroke and fill attributes and transformations (**K** – **O**).

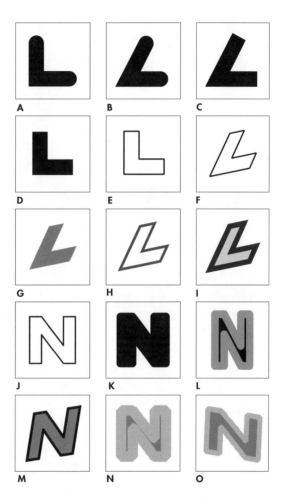

SHAPES COMBINING LINES WITH PLANE

124

A planar shape may lack detail (**A**). We can add one or more open paths, which may be straight, curved, angular, or looped, to its interior (**B**, **C**); to its outside edges (**D**, **E**); or to cross over it partially or completely (**F**, **G**). If the closed path is filled, open paths overlapping the fill can be stroked in white (**H**, **I**).

Open paths can remain loose if they are completely confined to the interior of the closed path (**J**, **K**).

F

G

H

I

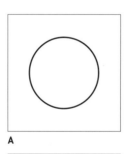

A

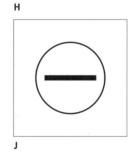

J

K

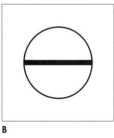

B

C

D

E

AGGREGATES

An aggregate results when two or more shapes are brought together and seen as a larger or more complex shape. Within an aggregate, the shapes may fuse with one another if they are not stroked but have the same fill (**A**), or overlap if they are stroked, or have different fills (**B**, **C**).

An aggregate may have loose shapes (**D**), negative shapes (**E**), shapes within shapes (**F**), or empty space completely surrounded by the shapes (**G**).

Overlapping planar shapes may be joined into a composite, with interpenetrated areas (**H**) (see the section in chapter 4 on joining shapes, page 50).

If all shapes in an aggregate are connected and filled, we can use the tracing tool to obtain a copy as one closed path, which may be assigned a new set of attributes (**I**).

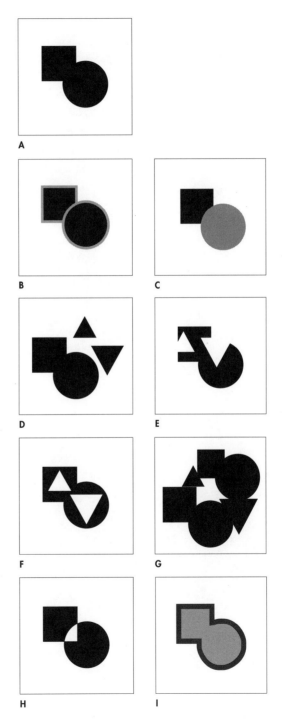

A

B

C

D

E

F

G

H

I

COMPONENTS AND UNITS

126

Shapes that constitute an aggregate are either components or units. They are components when they have different configurations. They are units when they show the same configuration.

Components of an aggregate should have something in common to attain unity. They may have the same line weight (**A**), other stroke attributes (**B**), fill attribute (**C**), size (**D**), or a combination of these qualities (**E**).

Units of an aggregate can be identical in every aspect (**F**), or may vary in stroke and fill combinations (**G – L**). Some may be rotated (**M**), reflected (**N**), uniformly scaled (**O**), disproportionately scaled (**P**), skewed (**Q**), or transformed with more than one tool (**R**).

Our examples show the components or units freely arranged to form the aggregate. They can also be aranged in a formal organization, which is the subject of the next chapter.

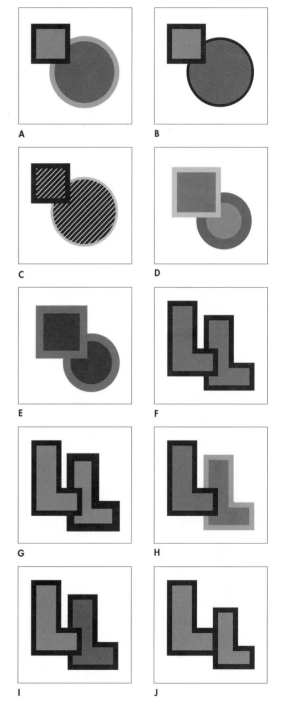

A

B

C

D

E

F

G

H

I

J

SUPERUNITS

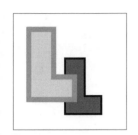

K

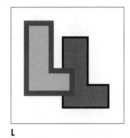

L

M

N

O

P

Q

R

We can use shapes, or shapes as units, to achieve a composition, without first gathering them as aggregates. We can have shapes as components or units to form one aggregate, and repeat the aggregates in a composition. Any aggregate that appears more than once, with or without transformation or variation, can be regarded as a *superunit*.

Two superunits can be arranged by simply bringing them together (**A**), rotating one 180 degrees (**B**), or reflecting one horizontally or vertically (**C**, **D**). A complicated composition can be accomplished with more superunits (**E** – **G**).

We can vary an aggregate to distinguish it from another by changing its attributes, size, proportion, and/or skewing (**H** – **K**), or just changing features of the individual components (**L** – **O**), rearranging their positions if necessary (**P**, **Q**).

1 2 7

128

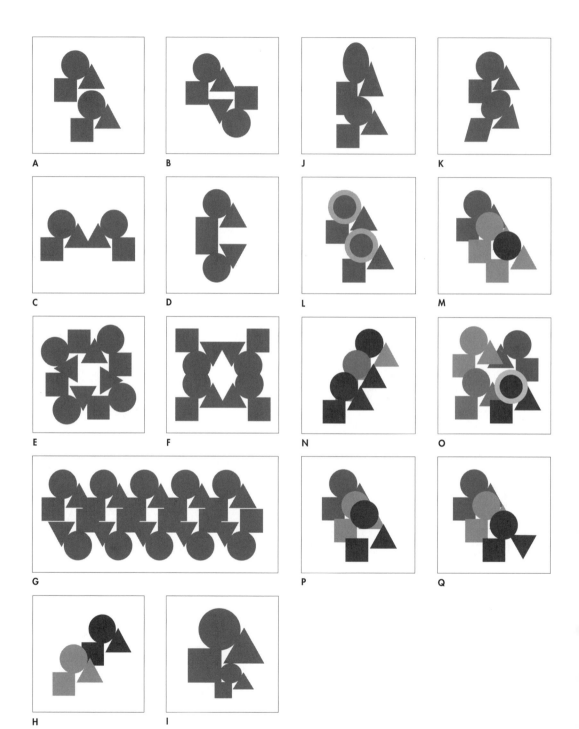

REPETITION AND VARIATIONS

Units or superunits that are straight copies of one original simply reflect the visual relationship of *repetition* (**A**). Sometimes it is desirable to introduce variations among the copies (**B**).

Severe variations, however, could dissociate the units or superunits completely and should be effected with discretion. When there are more than two units or superunits, we can have them showing a progressive change in line weight (**C, D**), shade of stroke (**E, F**), shade of fill (**G, H**), size (**I, J**), proportion (**K, L**), direction (**M, N**), position of elements or components (**O, P**), and/or skewing angle (**Q, R**). We may use the method of blending in some instances. If the arrangement follows the order of the change, the units or superunits thus exhibit a visual relationship of *gradation* (**S, T**). Disarranging the order achieves the visual relationship of *similarity* (**U, V**).

Gradation can also be attained with the progressive transformation of the edges of shapes (**W, X**). Similarity can be established with variation of pattern or texture, or with layering arrangements that are not or cannot be progressively effected (**Y, Z**).

A

B

C

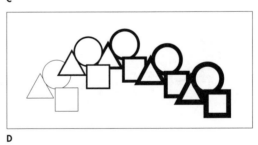

D

130

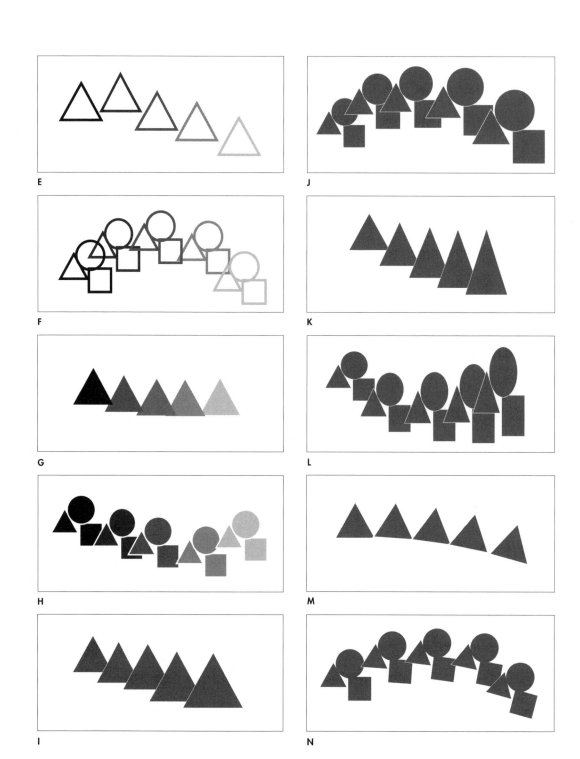

E

J

F

K

G

L

H

M

I

N

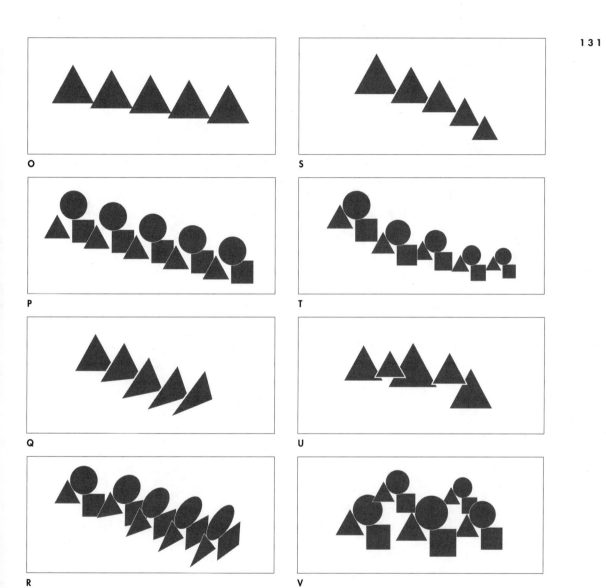

O

S

P

T

Q

U

R

V

132

W

Y

X

Z

SUGGESTED PROBLEMS

Try using a letter form and a geometric shape to form an aggregate, and obtain four distinctly different configurations through the variation or transformation of the components (**A** – **D**). Subsequently try developing the following compositions, each featuring only one chosen aggregate:

A

B

C

D

- Use the aggregate as a superunit four or more times, without any change, to show the visual relationship of repetition (**E**).
- Progressively vary the attributes to show the visual relationship of gradation (**F**).
- Progressively vary the positions and/or directions of the components comprising each aggregate to show the visual relationship of gradation (**G**).
- Rearrange any of the compositions that feature the visual relationship of gradation to show the relationship of similarity, changing the attributes of some components if desired (**H**).

134

E

G

F

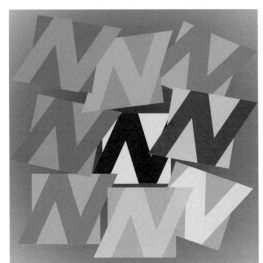

H

FORMAL ORGANIZATION

10

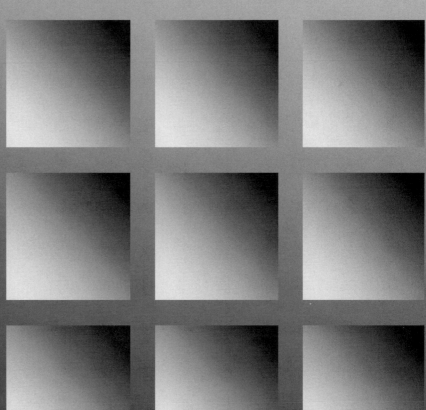

1 3 6

As discussed in the preceding chapter, shapes as components or units in an aggregate, or aggregates as superunits in a composition, can display visual relationships of repetition, gradation, and similarity.

Such relationships refer primarily to the general configurations and attributes of the units or superunits, which can be arranged freely without necessarily leading to formal organization.

Formal organization concerns the spatial distribution and alignment of the units or superunits to establish a sense of regularity.

Regularity may be the result of using one or more kinds of mathematical symmetry. These are translation, reflection, rotation, and dilation, and they form the basis of all kinds of formal organization.

TRANSLATION

Translation refers to shifting the position of a shape, aggregate, unit, or superunit, without changing its orientation or size. This can be achieved if we clone an original and subsequenly move the copy away from the original, which remains stationary and visible (**A**, **B**).

In formal organization, we may use *serial translation* to obtain, through power duplication, a range of units or superunits all equidistantly placed in a horizontal, vertical, or slanting linear arrangement. We need to use at least three units to establish a sequence, but we can use as many as desirable. They can be widely spread or closely related (**C**, **D**).

A linear arrangement of units can be translated again to form a planar arrangement, which may consist of two or more repetitions, obtainable also with power duplication (**E**, **F**).

If we do not want the units or superunits to have identical attributes, we can vary their strokes and fills to show a visual relationship of gradation (**G**, **H**) or similarity (**I**, **J**), without affecting the general effect of serial translation.

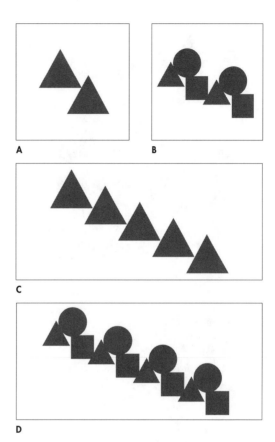

A

B

C

D

138

E

F

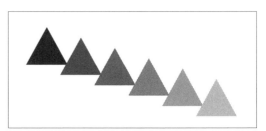

G

H

I

J

REFLECTION

A unit or superunit lying next to its reflected copy, with or without overlap, usually establishes bilateral symmetry, the kind of symmetry meant in our common understanding of the term (**A**, **B**). Between the unit and its reflected copy lies an imaginary axis.

We can reflect the unit along a horizontal or vertical axis after rotating it (**C**, **D**), or reflect it along a tilted axis without rotating it (**E**, **F**).

The original and its reflected copy form an aggregate, which can be further reflected to attain *serial reflection* (**G**, **H**). The operation can be repeated again in a larger, planar arrangement (**I**, **J**).

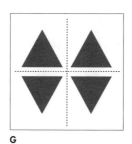

G

H

I

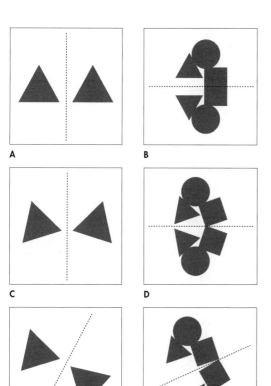

A

B

C

D

E

F

J

ROTATION

Rotation changes the orientation of a unit or super-unit. After cloning a unit or superunit, we can click with the rotating tool to locate a center of rotation, and subsequently drag with it to effect a rotating movement (**A**, **B**).

With power duplication, we can effect *serial rotation*, to have a partial or full revolution of the units or superunits (**C**, **D**). If the angle of rotation can be multiplied to obtain 360 degrees, a full revolution will show a perfect link between the first and the last of the series of units or superunits.

Location of the center of rotation is crucial to a satisfactory configuration. We may have to try a few times, with the center closer or farther away from the original, and compare the results (**E**, **F**). For better control, we can first group the original and its 180-degree rotated copy along an imaginary vertical axis, and, after cloning the group, use the associated dialog box to specify the angle of rotation. We then choose the *center of selection* as the center of rotation.

We can combine rotation with translation by rearranging rotated units or superunits in a row or column equidistantly (**G**, **H**). An *alignment* command may be available to help keep the arrangement precise. Alternatively, we can progressively rotate individual units or superunits after serial translation.

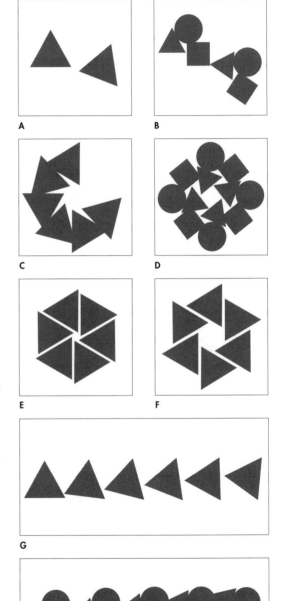

A

B

C

D

E

F

G

H

DILATION

Dilation refers to an increase in size, but we can use the term to denote any proportionate or disproportionate scale change of a unit or superunit. If the unit or superunit is grouped, scale change can be easily effected by dragging any object handle with the arrow tool.

For *serial dilation*, we may have to use a simple unit featuring a wide enclosure of space within a closed path, and specify vertical and horizontal scale changes in the dialog box associated with the scaling tool, choosing the center of selection as the center for scaling. This can produce a scaled copy on top of the original, and we can then proceed with power duplication to achieve progressive dilation in a concentric arrangement.

The series of units or superunits, however, must be stroked with a fine line and left unfilled so that they can be clearly visible (**A**, **B**). After the operation, we can reassign stroke and fill attributes, with gradation if desired, and we may have to rearrange the layering so that smaller ones are always on top of larger ones (**C**, **D**).

We can combine dilation with rotation while using power duplication (**E**, **F**). We can also combine dilation with translation by giving progressive scale change to individual units in a serial translation (**G**). This effect can be given to units or superunits that have complex configurations (**H**).

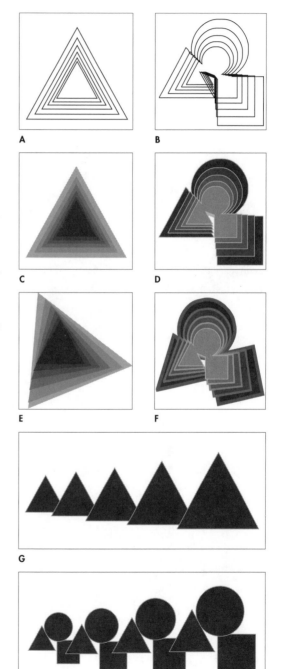

A

B

C

D

E

F

G

H

USING LETTER FORMS

To explore the different possibilities of formal organization, we can choose an existing letter form as a unit for translation, reflection, rotation, and dilation.

Letter forms actually represent a rather wide range of shapes, providing convenient starting points for the creation of interesting configurations. Our examples here demonstrate the use of the sans-serif letters H, R, P, V, and C and the serifed letter M to establish formally organized aggregates in different ways (**A – F**).

It is easy to see that some letter forms are bilaterally symmetrical shapes, some combine curvilinear and rectilinear elements, and some have semienclosed space for accommodating smaller shapes.

A

B

C

D

E

F

DIFFERENT VERSIONS OF A SHAPE

Any shape can undergo scale and attribute changes, modifications, and transformations, resulting in many variations, which are different *versions* of the same shape. If we use a shape as a unit for formal organization, we should know what versions are available.

To obtain possible versions of the letter N, for example, we can first give the shape proportionate and disproportionate scale changes (**A** – **D**). The shape may be stroked but not filled (**E** – **H**), but may also be stroked and filled in the same shade, resulting in a "fatter" configuration (**I**, **J**). It can look much thinner when stroked in white but filled with a shade (**K**, **L**). We can stroke and fill it in different shades (**M**, **N**) or patterns (**O**, **P**), and can combine shade and pattern in the attributes (**Q**, **R**).

Using round and beveled joins in the strokes produces further versions (**S**, **T**). Converting the letter into paths allows us to substitute points and move the point handles to effect more significant changes to the shape (**U**, **V**). Different fonts of the same letter provide many more versions (**W**, **X**). Any version may be skewed, reflected, or rotated before use (**Y**, **Z**).

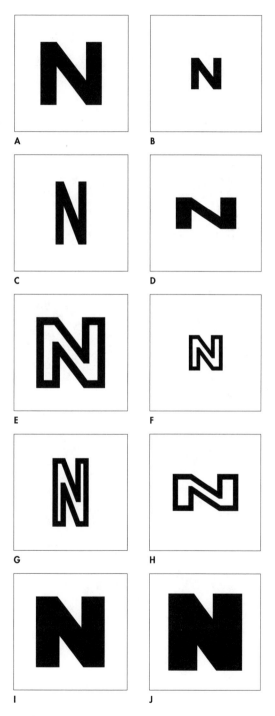

A

B

C

D

E

F

G

H

I

J

144

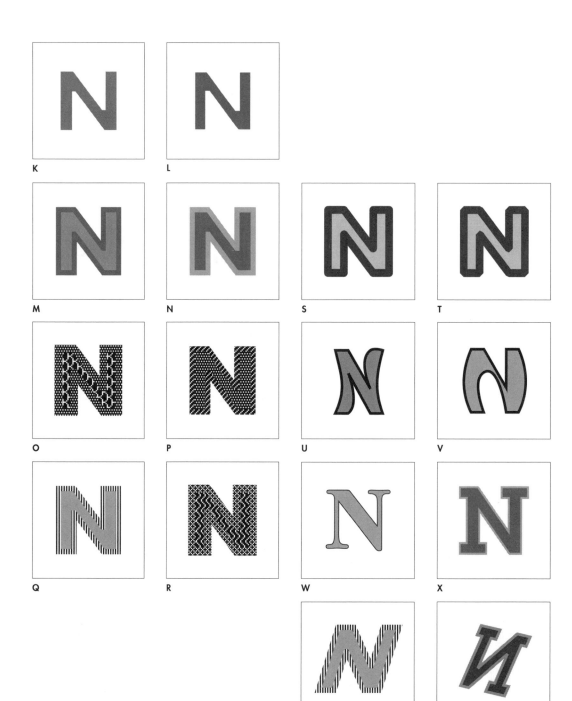

K

L

M

N

S

T

O

P

U

V

Q

R

W

X

Y

Z

ARRANGING TWO UNITS

To create a basic design, we can construct an
aggregate using units based on one chosen letter
form. Each such aggregate generally features one
particular version of the unit, but may sometimes
feature more than one version.

With two units, we can create numerous different
arrangements with simple translation (**A – I**),
reflection (**J – M**), and dilation (**N**).

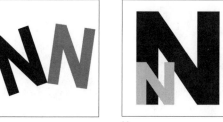

G

H

I

J

A

B

K

L

C

D

M

N

E

F

ARRANGING THREE UNITS

146

With three units, we may be able to attain a formal organization that displays more obvious regularity. We can have serial translation (**A**, **B**), serial rotation (**C** – **E**), serial translation combined with rotation (**F**), serial translation with dilation (**G** – **I**), and serial translation with rotated units that are progressively skewed (**J**).

Serial translation can include a reflected unit, but regularity could be slightly disrupted (**K**, **L**).

G

H

I

J

A

B

K

L

C

D

E

F

ARRANGING FOUR UNITS

Four units can be seen either as a group of four or two groups of two each. They can form a full revolution with right-angled rotation.

With four units in row, we can have serial translation in a linear arrangement (**A**). With two rows of two units in each row, the resultant configuration displays planar arrangement (**B**). Serial reflection is possible with four units (**C**). Different arrangements can be explored with serial rotation (**D** – **G**). Serial dilation can be combined with translation (**H**), as well as with progressive skewing (**I**).

We can have two units of one version and two units of another version working together and still achieve formal organization (**J** – **M**).

D

E

F

G

H

I

A

B

J

K

C

L

M

ARRANGING SIX UNITS

148

Six units can be seen as one group of six, two groups of three each, or three groups of two each. They can form a full revolution with 60-degree or 120-degree rotation.

For an aggregate, six units in a row or column may seem too long. In this case, we can arrange them in two or three rows or columns in a planar arrangement with serial translation (**A** – **C**).

We can combine serial translation with reflection (**D** – **F**), serial rotation with translation (**G**), serial dilation with translation (**H**, **I**), and serial dilation with reflection and translation (**J**).

A

B

C

D

E

F

G

H

I

J

ARRANGING EIGHT UNITS

Eights units can can appear in one group of eight, two groups of four each, or four groups of two each. They can form a full revolution with 45-degree or right-angled rotation.

We can have two rows of units in serial translation (**A**), which may be combined with reflection (**B**). We can have individual units, or groups of two units of the same or different versions, in serial rotation (**C** – **I**), and we can repeat four units in serial dilation (**J**).

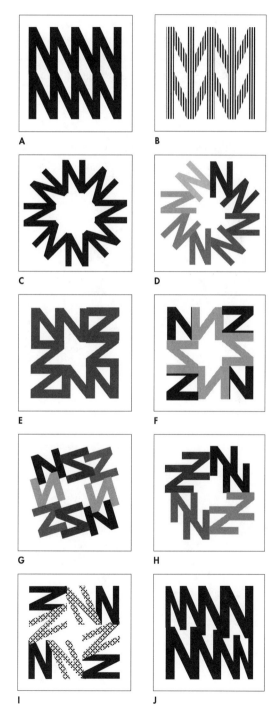

A

B

C

D

E

F

G

H

I

J

ARRANGING NINE UNITS

Nine units can easily form a planar arrangement, with three rows each containing three units in serial translation (**A**, **B**). Each row may include a reflected version (**C**, **D**). We can have three units in serial rotation and repeat them in a further serial rotation (**E**).

Each unit or each row may be skewed in alternate directions (**F**, **G**). Translation, rotation, and dilation can all be combined in a planar arrangement (**H**).

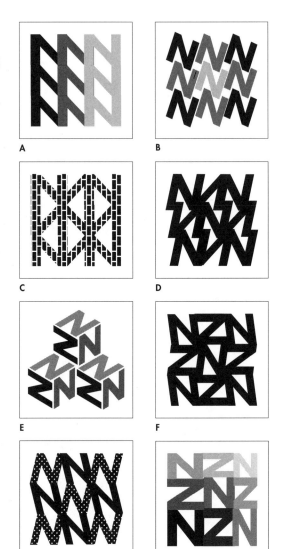

A

B

C

D

E

F

G

H

AGGREGATES AS SUPERUNITS

Arrangements of two, three, four, six, eight, or nine units are aggregates. Aggregates can be compositions by themselves, or may be repeated, if desired, with or without variations, as superunits in a composition.

Before applying the concepts of translation, reflection, rotation, and dilation, any chosen aggregate (**A**) can be assigned new attributes (**B**), disproportionately scaled (**C**), or skewed and subsequently reflected or rotated (**D**).

Superunits may have regularly varied attributes when they are in serial translation or other forms of formal organization (**E – G**).

One or more aggregates establishing a composition can be placed on black, gray, patterned, or gradient backgrounds to facilitate the effective use of white-stroked or white-filled units (**H – K**).

E

F

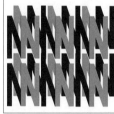

G

H

I

J

A

B

C

D

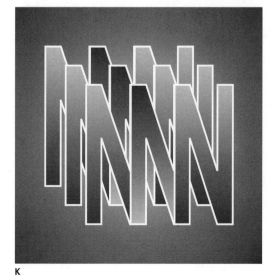

K

ADDING LAYERS AND SHADOWS

152

To add a feeling of depth, one or more layers in a different shade or pattern can be added behind an aggregate. The layers may be of the same size (**A**), or slightly larger (**B**), taller (**C**), or wider (**D**).

If there is only one layer, the layer may appear as a shadow of the aggregate. It can be filled with black, gray, or a gradient (**E** – **G**). If we skew the layer, or skew the aggregate and the layer in different directions, the suggestion of shadow can be even more convincing (**H**, **I**).

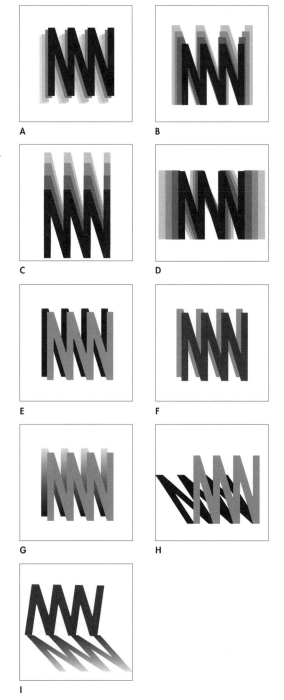

A

B

C

D

E

F

G

H

I

SUGGESTED PROBLEMS

Try choosing a letter form to use as the basis of a unit for developing into an aggregate. Examine all possible versions, and arrange two or more units, applying the different kinds of mathematical symmetry to attain formal organization, with shadow effects (**A – D**).

Subsequently try using one resultant aggregate as a superunit, on a white or shaded background, in serial translation, regularly varying attributes of mecessary (**E – H**).

B

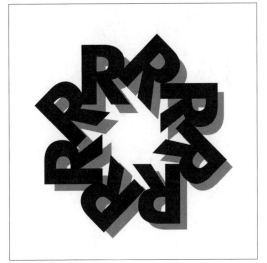

C

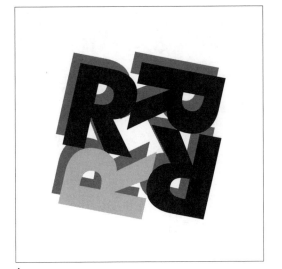

A

D

154

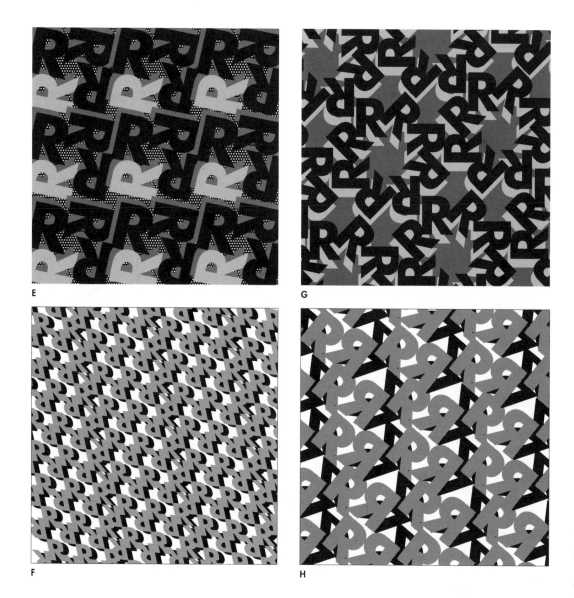

E

G

F

H

11

156

In formal organization, we may rely basically on power duplication and alignment commands to achieve regular arrangements of units or superunits. In addition, all regular arrangements can be accomplished with reference to an underlying structure.

A structure is a grid that divides the design area or the background into subdivisions. Shapes, units, aggregates, or superunits may be placed at intersections of the structural lines or within the subdivisions defined by the structural lines.

Most draw programs provide vertical and horizontal rulers, from which we can drag *ruler guides* for constructing a right-angled linear grid parallel to the edges of the document window. Some draw programs may also provide a customizable grid composed of dots. With ruler guides and dotted grids, elements and shapes can be "snapped" and shifted automatically to proper positions after activating corresponding commands.

A predesigned structural grid used as a template for manual positioning is often necessary for compositions of a complex nature.

TYPES OF STRUCTURES

We have used the mathematical concepts of translation, reflection, rotation, and dilation to achieve formal organization. Naturally, the different types of structures are also based on these concepts.

Structures fall into four easily distinguishable types. These are repetition structures, gradation structures, radiation structures, and concentricity structures.

The basic configuration of a *repetition structure* could be represented by a grid composed of five vertical and five horizontal lines equidistantly spaced, making a total of sixteen squares in four repeated rows or columns (**A**). This structure accommodates units or superunits in serial translation (**B**).

Progressively narrowing or expanding the space between the lines converts a repetition structure into a *gradation structure* (**C**). Units or superunits should be in serial translation as well as in serial dilation, probably with a gradual changing of their proportions to fit the varying shapes and sizes of the subdivisions (**D**).

The basic configuration of a *radiation structure* is circular, constructed with rotated lines at 15-degree increments (**E**). This structure accommodates units or superunits in serial rotation (**F**).

A *concentricity structure* can be represented by a series of concentric rings in a circular configuration (**G**). This structure accommodates serially dilated units or superunits that are superimposed upon or nested within one another (**H**).

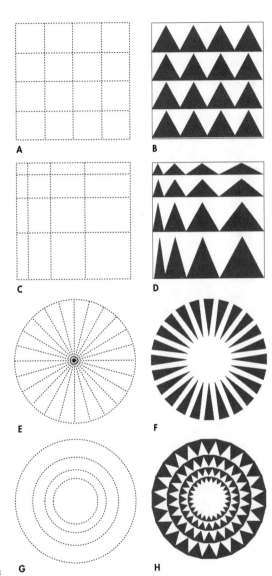

A

B

C

D

E

F

G

H

VISUAL ORDER

Each type of structure leads to the establishment of a particular kind of visual order. A repetition structure normally expresses the visual order of repetition, a gradation structure the order of gradation, a radiation structure the order of radiation, and a concentricity structure the order of concentricity.

Note that the structure primarily determines spatial relationship of units or superunits, among which there is the visual relationship of repetition, gradation, or similarity that effects the visual order in combination with the structure.

We may use a repetition structure to express the visual order of gradation by having the units or superunits showing gradual changes of size, attributes, orientation, or transformation (**A – D**). Radiation and concentric structures can also express the order of gradation to some extent (**E**, **F**).

Any type of structure can accommodate units that have a visual relationship of similarity or that show irregular variations. In such instances, the design does not establish any visual order of strict regularity.

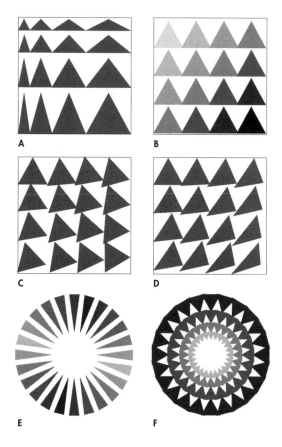

A   B

C   D

E   F

REPETITION STRUCTURES

A repetition structure makes possible the arrangement of units or superunits in equal distance horizontally as well as vertically. The horizontal and vertical distances can be different and should be adjusted to suit the shape of the unit or superunit.

A wide shape, such as the letter M, definitely requires more horizontal space than a narrow shape, such as the letter J. Units can overlap considerably in a row, but rows can remain separate in their vertical repetitions (**A**, **B**). A unit can be rotated slightly before horizontal serial translation, and this may allow a shape such as the letter L to move a lot closer to its repetitions without overlapping (**C**).

If we use the letter H as a unit forming a row, the rows can be repeated straight down, or staggered so that every other row fits into the open spaces of the units (**D**). If we first arrange the letter H in a column, we can rotate the letter before use, tuck all the letters in the column, and repeat the column in ascending or descending steps (**E**).

A triangular shape, such as the letter V, can alternate with its reflected version in a horizontal row (**F**). Two or more units can constitute an aggregate for use as a superunit in a repetition structure (**G**). Variations of attributes can always be introduced at regular intervals (**H**).

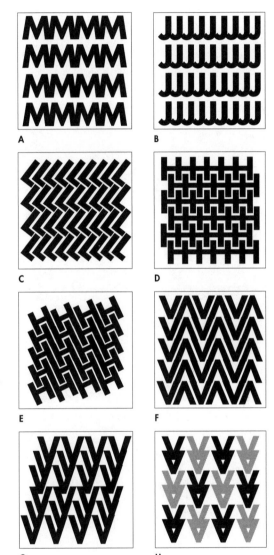

A

B

C

D

E

F

G

H

GRADATION STRUCTURES

160

A gradation structure consists of a number of subdivisions, which show progressive size and/or proportion changes horizontally, vertically, or in both directions. Units within the subdivisions may remain unchanged in their size or proportions and just show increasing or decreasing distance from one another as they spread (**A**).

Each unit can also change in size and proportion to fit the subdivision it occupies. We can start with the largest to be featured. After cloning it, we can scale the copy vertically 100 percent but horizontally 90 percent, move it sideways, effect power duplication to get a row of gradually narrowing units extended in one direction, and repeat the process to get the row extended in the opposite direction. The spacing of units may need adjustment. Repeating the row downward results in a design showing horizontal gradation (**B**).

Vertical gradation can be achieved in a similar manner. To achieve a design featuring both vertical and horizontal gradations, we can use one horizontal row obtained in the method just described, clone, move, and scale each unit vertically 90 percent and horizontally 100 percemt, effect power duplication to obtain a vertical column above the row, and repeat the process to extend the column below the row (**C**). If the largest unit occupies the center of the design, it represents the climax in the order of gradation. We can reverse the size arrangements to have the smallest unit as the climax, if desired (**D**).

A

B

C

D

RADIATION STRUCTURES

Space provided for each unit in a radiation structure is often in a wedge shape, narrow and pointed at one end and wide at the other. A squarish unit may fit well if there are only four rotations (**A**). Otherwise, overlapping is almost inevitable if we do not want a composition with loosely scattered shapes.

There are three factors affecting a radiation structure: the center of radiation, the distance of units from the center, and the orientation of the units before rotation. Units can overlap the center, touch one another at the center, or revolve around the center, which then becomes an open area (**B – D**). The center becomes a wider open area with units moving away from it (**E**). Different orientations of the unit may result in different designs (**F, G**).

Starting with an original and a copy already rotated 180 degrees, we can place the two units on opposite sides of an imaginary vertical line, move the units farther apart or closer to get a midpoint as the center of rotation, and shift the units correspondingly to the left and right sides of the line to establish their orientation towards the center. After the arrangement, we can clone and rotate with subsequent power duplication to attain a full revolution, achieving results that may be close to our expectations (**H**).

To fit the wedge shape of a subdivision more properly, we can stretch or skew the unit, or have large and small units forming a superunit for rotation (**I, J**).

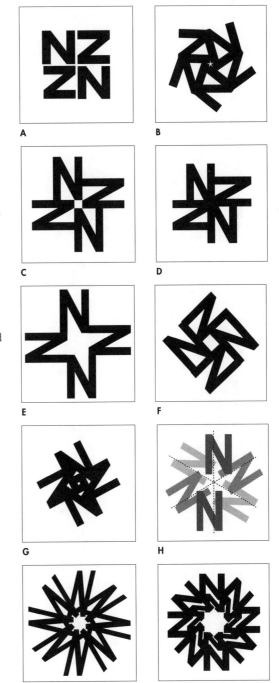

A

B

C

D

E

F

G

H

I

J

CONCENTRICITY STRUCTURES

A concentricity structure shows superimposed units in expanding or contracting multiple layers. Each unit maps out its area of subdivision. We can use this type of structure for any filled or unfilled shape (**A** – **D**).

We can also first rotate a unit to form a continuous ring of shapes. After cloning it, we can then scale down the copy, say about 80 percent, probably also rotate it 5 to 10 degrees, and use power duplication to obtain further scaled down and rotated copies. Each layer may have to be assigned different shades if the layers overlap (**E**, **F**).

Alternatively, we can translate a unit to form a row, have rotated rows to form a square or polygonal configuration, and use power duplication to obtain progressively reduced layers piling on top of one another, reassigning attributes if necessary (**G**, **H**).

Simple geometric shapes such as circles, ellipses, squares or rectangles can be effectively used in concentricity structures. Units gradually diminished in scale can display gradual changes in proportion, size, and attributes (**I** – **V**).

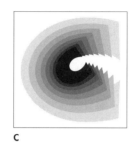

C

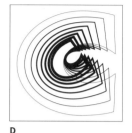

D

E

F

G

H

A

B

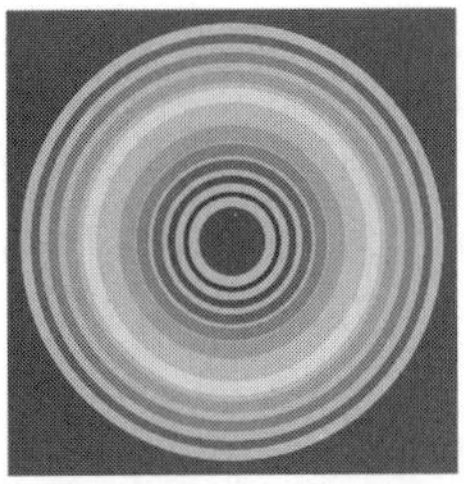

I

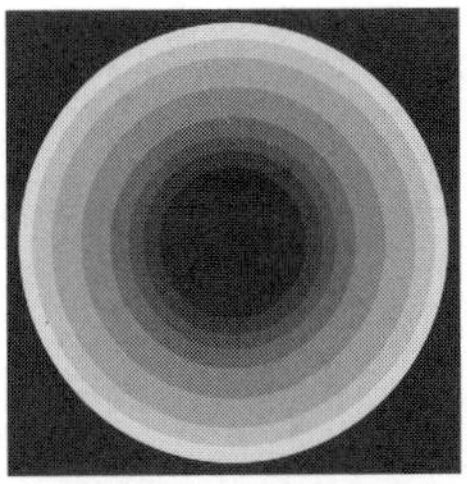

J

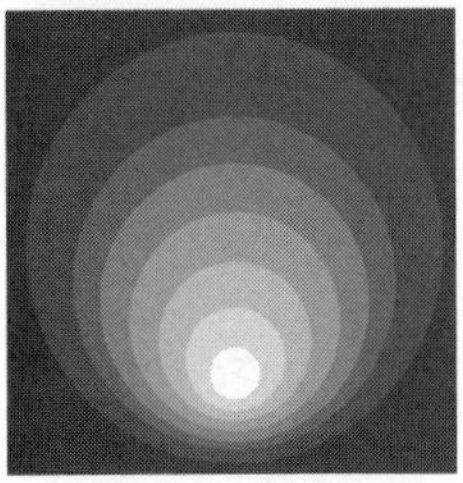

K

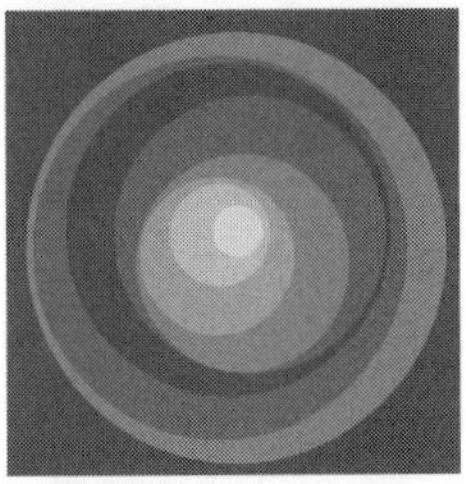

L

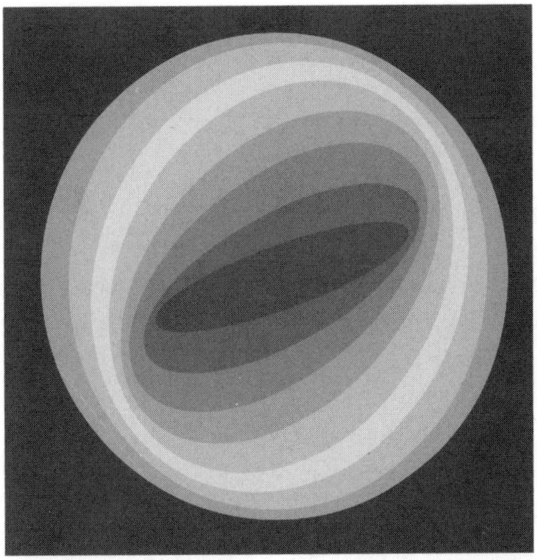

P

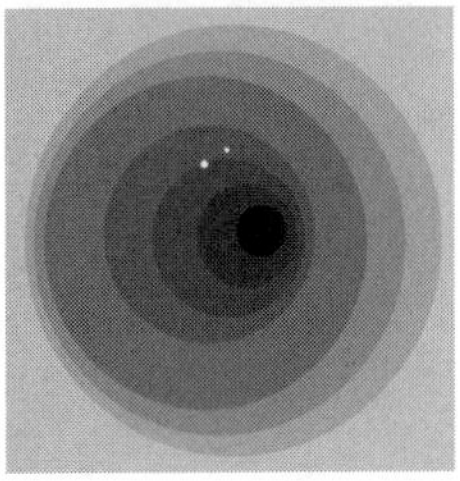

M

N

Q

R

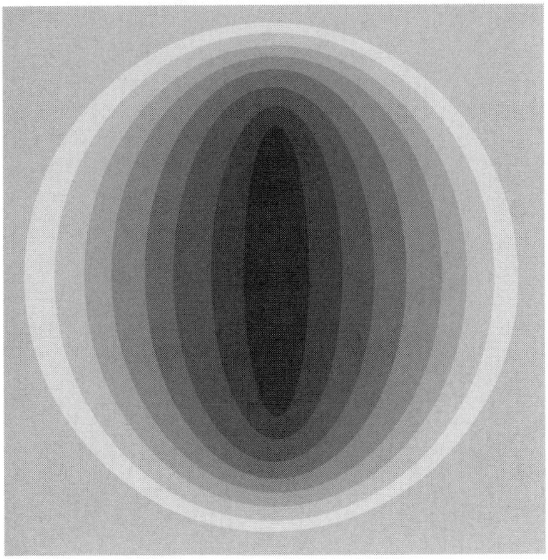

O

S

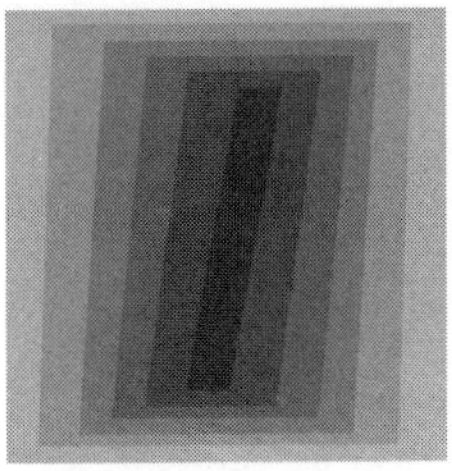

T

U

V

THREE LEVELS OF CONSTRUCTION

164

Any of the four types of structure can have three levels of construction: the point level, the line level, and the plane level.

The point level of construction is the most common. We can proceed with one single shape as a unit, or one aggregate as a superunit, and effect translation, rotation, or dilation as necessary to establish a structure expressing a particular kind of visual order (**A**, **B**).

On the line level, we can have a row of units or superunits that is not straight but zigzag, curved, or otherwise distorted, and use this as a large aggregate for repetition, gradation, or rotation (**C** – **F**), or for forming a squared or polygonal ring for concentricity (**G**). The units can be progressively or rhythmically spaced or rotated (**H**).

On the plane level, we can arrange a number of units or superunits, individually or in rows, to form a plane that may be regarded as one very large aggregate. For repetition and gradation, this aggregate should be a square, rectangle, rhombus, or parallelogram (**I**, **J**). For radiation, it should be a wedge (**K**). For concentricity, aggregates as dilated layers must be arranged in different shades (**L**).

C

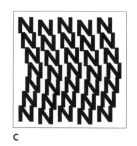

D

E

F

G

H

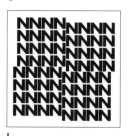

I

J

A

B

K

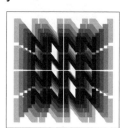

L

SUBDIVISIONS IN STRUCTURES

Some compositions may require the use of specially designed structural grids used as a template on a
nonprinting layer to guide units or superunits to
their exact locations and orientations.

Subdivisions in a repetition structure can be triangles, trapeziums, or hexagons, instead of squares or
rectangles (**A – C**). The straight lines in a repetition,
gradation, or radiation structure can be reshaped as
angular or curvilinear lines (**D – G**).

D

E

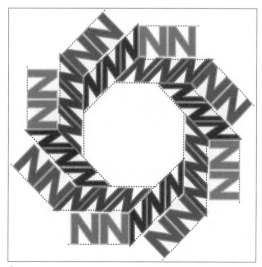

F

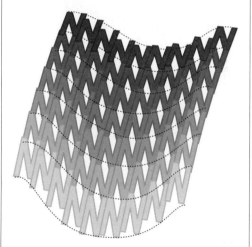

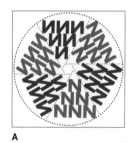

A

B

C

G

FITTING UNITS TO SUBDIVISIONS

166

Units or superunits may be of a proper size and proportion to fit a subdivision, or may be scaled proportionately or disproportionately to fit the subdivision. When a unit or a superunit cannot be contained completely within the boundary of a subdivision, we can allow it to intrude into adjacent subdivisions or crop it to fit.

The cropping of any shape or aggregate can be done with a *clipping path*, a method usually available in a draw program. We can trace the shape of the subdivision on the template, move the unit or superunit into the traced shape, and cut the selected unit or superunit with the *cut* command. Subsequently we can select the traced shape, which is now empty, and use the *paste inside* command to place the unit or superunit cropped to the boundary of the traced shape.

The traced shape and its clipped contents together form a new superunit for repeated use. We can stroke and fill the traced shape if necessary, and can use the new superunit with or without transformation in a repetition (**A**), gradation (**B**), or radiation (**C**) structure.

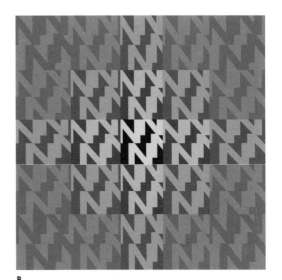

B

C

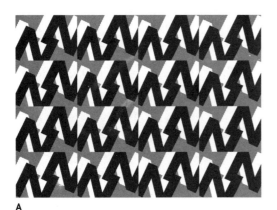

A

POSITIVE/NEGATIVE ALTERNATIONS

Subdivisions can have different background shades. In a black and white design, we can use black shapes on white ground and white shapes on black ground, to show positive/negative alternations.

Before placement of units in the subdivisions, a repetition structure with such alternations may look like a checkerboard. We can create this checkerboard on screen with rows of alternating black and white squares or rectangles (**A**). White units can then be placed in the black areas, and black units in the white areas, of this checkerboard pattern (**B**). Each unit may have to be cropped by a clipping path to fit the area. Gradual changes in the positions of these units can suggest the order of gradation (**C**).

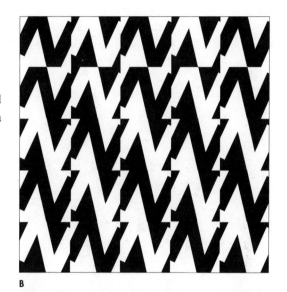

B

A

C

REPEATING THE STRUCTURES

Any structure, complete with all fitted units or superunits, can be repeated, with or without rescaling or rotation, to form a larger composition.

We can repeat one entire repetition structure, with rescaling, to suggest the order of repetition (**A**) or gradation (**B**). We can use a clipping path to clip one part of a repetition, gradation, radiation, or concentricity structure for repetition and/or rotation (**C** – **H**). A radiation structure may be clipped and repeated without including its center (**I**).

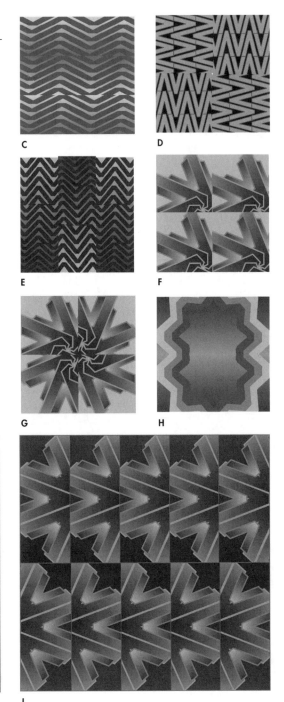

C

D

E

F

G

H

A

B

I

SUGGESTED PROBLEMS

Try choosing a letter form as the basis for a unit or a superunit to develop a series of compositions:

- Use individual units in a repetition structure to attain the visual order of repetition (**A**).
- Use superunits, each consisting of two or three units, in a repetition structure to attain the order of gradation (**B**).
- Use gradually changing individual units in a gradation structure to attain the order of horizontal or vertical gradation (**C**).
- Use three gradually changing units arranged in a row or on a plane to form a superunit for rotation in a radiation structure (**D**).
- Use six rows of units forming a hexagonal ring and progressively reduce the size of the ring to attain the order of concentricity (**E**).
- Choose one of the resultant structures, clip a part, and repeat the clipped part in a larger composition, with or without rescaling or rotation (**F**).

A

B

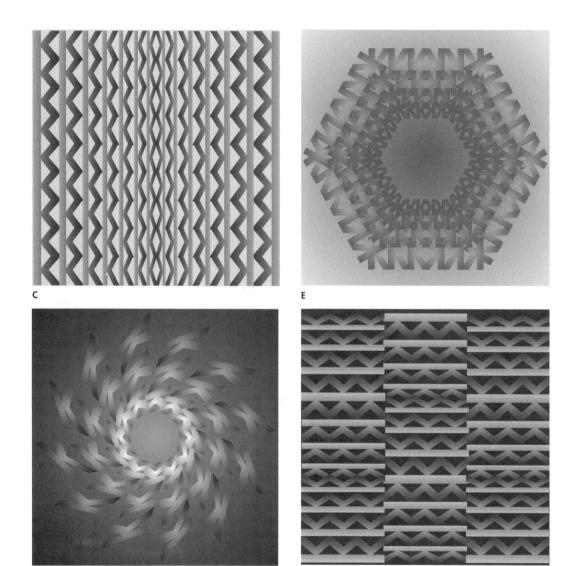

C

E

D

F

12

172

As we have seen, units or superunits in serial translation, serial reflection, serial rotation, and/or serial dilation, establishing a repetition structure, a gradation structure, a radiation structure, or a concentricity structure, express a kind of visual order with full regularity.

While strict regularity can ensure unity and equilibrium in a composition, it can sometimes impose rigidity and monotony. The presence of variations may help to bring freshness to the design. Variations can occur regularly, but can also happen singularly or sporadically, presenting some irregularity in the composition.

Irregularity displayed by a few units introduces *anomaly*, changing any formal organization to semiformal. The composition may still generally show the visual order of repetition, gradation, radiation, or concentricity.

To increase irregularity, we can seek informal organization, with disfiguration of shapes, units, aggregates, or superunits, with *deconstruction* of the structure. We may try to design without conscious reference to visual order of any kind.

ANOMALY

Anomaly is just a diversion from overall regularity. It should occur sparingly in a composition, and could be restricted to one unit.

To achieve anomaly, we can have the unit showing a different attribute (**A**), size (**B**), proportion (**C**), position (**D**), or orientation (**E**), among repeated identical units formally arranged. We can also reflect (**F**), skew (**G**), or crop (**H**) the unit, turn it into a negative (**I**), or replace it with another shape (**J**).

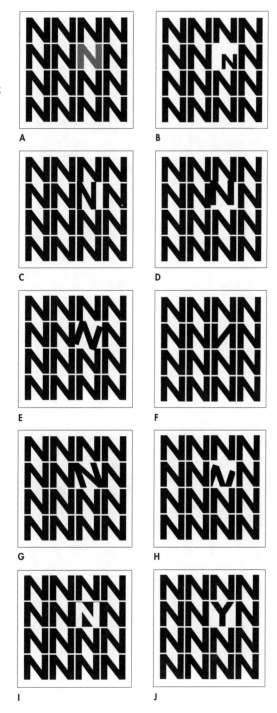

A

B

C

D

E

F

G

H

I

J

ANOMALY WITH PROMINENCE

174

An anomalous unit normally introduces a subtle accentuation. It can also be given considerable prominence to establish a focal point in the composition. In extreme cases, it can even assert an overwhelming presence.

The anomalous unit can be several times larger than the regular units (**A**). Contrast of size can be combined with other kinds of contrasts (**B**). The unit can be as large as the entire composition (**C, D**).

ANOMALOUS UNITS IN A COMPOSITION

When one single unit shows diversion from regularity, anomaly is effected only on the point level (see the section on three levels of construction in the preceding chapter). We can have an entire row, a column, a string, or a ring of units showing diversion, and effect anomaly on the line level (**A – H**). Within the row or column, the units may be varied (**I**).

An area of units in a composition can become anomalous (**J – M**), and the anomalous units may also be varied (**N**). We can superimpose duplicated units or another shape on that area, using the join elements command to attain the effect of interpenetration (**O, P**).

A few anomalous units can be scattered in different parts of the composition, and they can show the same diversion from general regularity (**Q, R**), or different diversions, with one anomalous unit assuming a stronger dominance (**S, T**).

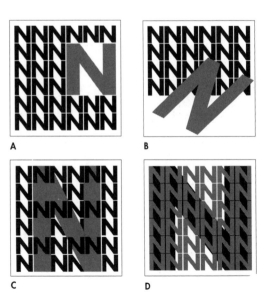

A

B

C

D

A

B

K

L

C

D

M

N

E

F

O

P

G

H

Q

R

I

J

S

T

ANOMALY AND SIMILARITY

176

When more than half of the units show the same diversion or different diversions from general regularity, they can no longer be regarded as anomalous units but instead, mixed with all other units in the composition, establish a visual relationship of similarity (**A**, **B**).

Units that shift in position may cause disruption to the structure (**C** – **E**). We can crop such units with clipping paths, restraining them within structural subdivisions, to maintain strict formal organization (**F** – **H**).

B

C

D

E

F

G

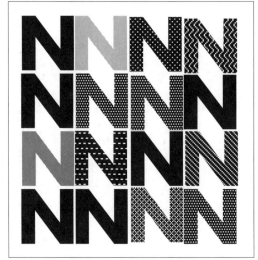

A

H

STRUCTURAL REORGANIZATION

Instead of creating anomaly among units, we can introduce anomaly to a portion of the structure. Changes in structure lead to corresponding changes in the units.

Structural anomaly should encompass a considerably large area to be effective. If the anomalous portion extends to half of the composition, it leads to structural reorganization.

In a repetition structure, as rows of units extend into a certain area, the arrangement might shift from a horizontal direction to a slanting direction or into a zigzag manner (**A**, **B**). Four rows of units in the left section may become six or more rows (**C**), or show uniform or gradual change of size or proportion (**D**) in the right section.

A radiation structure may have a third or half of the composition reorganized, showing uniform or gradual change in the angle of rotation (**E**, **F**).

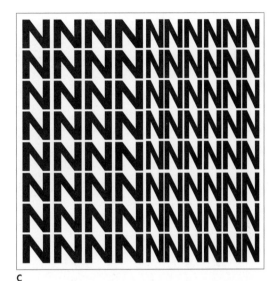

C

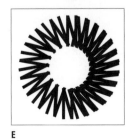

D

A

B

E

F

DISFIGURATION OF UNITS

178

Disfiguration is the distortion, deformation, deface-
ment, or breaking-up of the general shape of a
unit, to the extent that the unit can become almost
unrecognizable.

In a draw program, we can replace or move points
and handles of any number of units, or effect
extreme disproportionate scaling and skewing,
with rotation and reflection, to achieve the effect
of disfiguration (**A**, **B**). All disfigured units may stay
in locations defined by the structure, but the structural arrangement may become unclear.

To break up any unit into two or more parts, we
can use a clipping path to clip a unit after it is
cloned, and place the clipped portion in the same
location with some disalignment (**C**). We can clip
an area covering several units and clip more than
one area in a composition, rotating each clipped
area if necessary (**D**).

Actually, this way of breaking up units is more easily
accomplished in a paint program (see the section
in chapter 7 on breaking up the image, page 97).
Painted images may subsequently require editing
as SuperBits or retracing to improve their resolution.

A

B

C

D

DECONSTRUCTING REPETITION

Deconstruction of any structure can be done on the point level, the line level, and the plane level. The purpose of deconstruction is to disarrange regularly positioned units in the structure.

Deconstructing a repetition structure on the point level, we can move most of the units individually away from their original locations, adding or deleting any if necessary. After moving, we can also change their attributes, orientations, size, or proportions, or effect transformation or disfiguration, as desired (**A** – **C**).

On the line level, we can move, instead of individual units, entire rows or columns of grouped units. Dense conglomeration caused by heavy overlapping can be relieved by varying the fills (**D**) or by stroking the units in white (**E**). We can effect reflection, scale change, or transformation, if necessary (**F**).

On the plane level, we can group a number of units in an area and move or rotate the group with or without scale change or transformation (**G**, **H**). We can use any appropriate tool to make a shape for use as a clipping path to crop an area that can be moved, rotated, and filled with any appropriate shade (**I**). ·

The three levels of deconstruction can be combined to get individual units, rows, and fragmented areas working together in a composition (**J**).

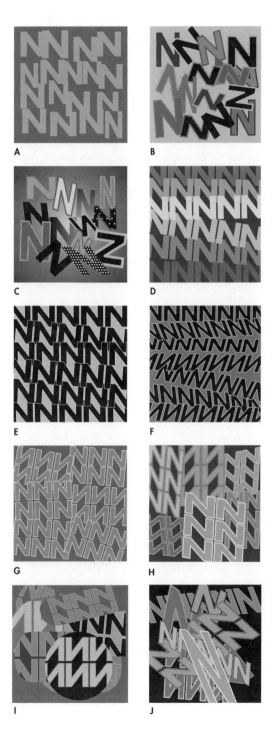

DECONSTRUCTING GRADATION

180

Starting with a composition consisting of a gradation structure, we can shift the positions of individual units—adding, deleting, rotating, reflecting, transforming, or changing attributes if necessary. Deconstruction here is on the point level (**A**, **B**).

Deconstructing the gradation structure on the line or plane level is similar to the way we deconstruct any repetition structure (**C** – **F**).

In all instances, the order of gradation is only disrupted and should not be completely demolished, to have the sense of gradual change still remaining vaguely apparent after disorganization.

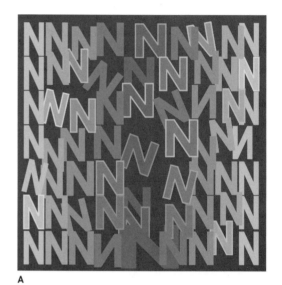

A

B

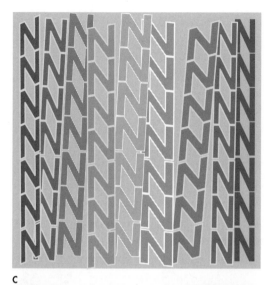

C

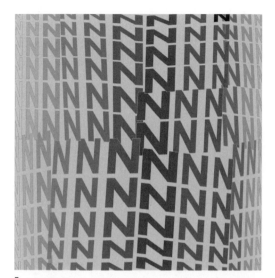

E

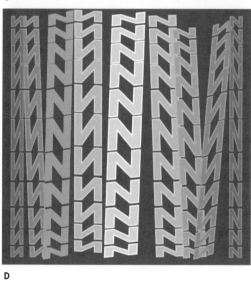

D

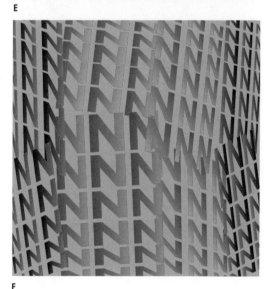

F

DECONSTRUCTING RADIATION

182

Deconstructing a radiation structure on the point level, we can move, rotate, reflect, rescale, or transform individual units and can change attributes (**A**, **B**).

If the radiation structure consists of a string of units that have been grouped and rotated, we can move each string and make changes to effect deconstruction on the line level (**C**, **D**).

We can select, group, and move any section or area of the radiation structure, or use clipping paths to slice and cut, to accomplish deconstruction on the plane level (**E**, **F**).

A

B

C

E

D

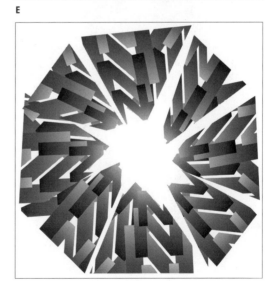

F

DECONSTRUCTING CONCENTRICITY

184

A concentricity structure featuring one unit in expanding or contracting concentric layers can be changed by moving, rotating, and transforming some or all of the layers as we effect deconstruction on the point level (**A**). If the structure consists of rings of units, then each individual unit may be moved, rotated, or transformed (**B**).

In deconstruction on the line level, the entire string of units can be moved, rotated, or transformed (**C**, **D**).

On the plane level, we can divide, with or without using clipping paths, the composition into separate areas that can be moved, rotated, or transformed during deconstruction (**E**, **F**).

A

B

C

E

D

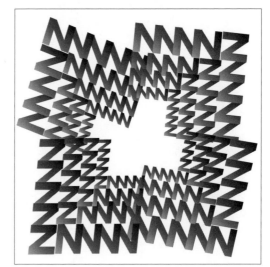

F

DECONSTRUCTING TYPE

186

When legibility is not the main concern, type as letters or single words may be deconstructed to attain specific effects of visual expression.

Individual letters of a word can be moved, rotated, reflected, rescaled, transformed, given new attributes, or shown in different fonts (**A**, **B**). An entire word can be shown in any orientation, joined to curved or angular paths, widely spaced, or tightly crammed (**C**, **D**).

We can have lines and shapes in white or any shade placed on top of some of the characters or the entire word, covering or hiding them partially (**E**, **F**). We can use clipping paths to break up the word or any character in the word (**G**, **H**).

If a paint program is used, we can effect disfiguration with pencil, brush, airbrush, smudge, eraser, lasso and marquee tools, and explore with patterns, textures, and gradients in different transfer modes (**I** – **L**).

C

D

E

F

G

H

I

J

A

B

K

L

SUGGESTED PROBLEMS

Try developing four pairs of designs encompassing repetition, gradation, radiation, and concentricity structures, and showing in each pair the regular structure and its deconstruction (**A – H**).

In addition, use the word "FRAGMENT," stressing the effects of disfiguration and general deconstruction, in a draw program (**I**, **J**) and, if possible, also in a paint program (**K**, **L**).

E

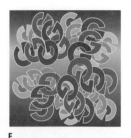

F

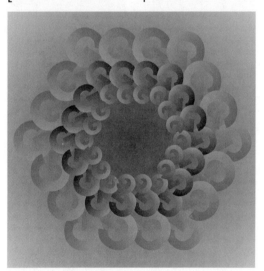

G

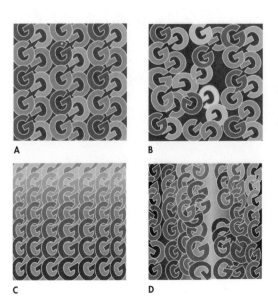

A

B

C

D

H

1 8 8

I

J

K

L

3

DON
GLA
INO

190

A design can be an isolated, scalable shape or aggregate that can be used anywhere. It can also be a composition in a fixed shape and size, with elements and shapes interacting with one another on a background.

A composition is confined to a surface and is restrained within the edges of the surface. The edges provide the composition a *frame of reference* and determine its overall configuration and dimensions.

A composition may also be seen as the incorporation of different visual entities coming from various sources. It frequently includes types as titles or texts for communication.

Communication is an important aspect of visual design. Shapes and aggregates may relate to our daily experience and can express meaning and meanings. Type that can be read may also communicate visually as shapes.

COMPOSITION AND COMMUNICATION

FRAME OF REFERENCE

A design printed on paper takes its frame of reference from the edges of the paper on which it appears. The edges mark off a border, within which space opens up like a stage, embodying voidness and depth, and outside which nothing can happen.

Paper is usually trimmed in a square or rectangular shape (**A**, **B**), whether as a single sheet or one page of a book. It may be specially cut in a circular, polygonal, or any other shape to meet particular requirements (**C – F**). A composition must work with the shape of its frame of reference.

Within the edges of the paper, margins are sometimes present, and they reduce the active area of the composition. A visible frame may be drawn to emphasize the frame of reference and distinguish clearly space inside and outside the composition, and its visual attributes actually become an integral part of the composition (**G**, **H**).

Designs from other sources may be imported to a single page, and each of these is itself a mini-composition. This is the case on the pages of this book, where all diagrams or illustrations are separate compositions, which may be surrounded with a square or rectangular linear frame in black.

Adjacent pages of a book, pamphlet, or brochure may form a continuous spread which is a composition appearing in folded sections (**I**).

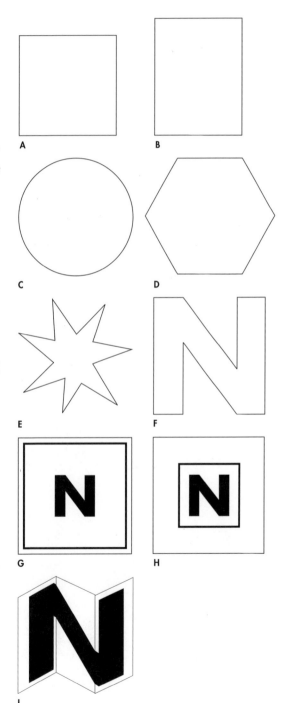

RELATIVE SIZE OF A SHAPE

192

Any shape or aggregate, once visualized on a surface, has a physical size. When it is seen within a frame of reference, it also acquires a relative size. Physical size is measurable in an absolute value. Relative size refers to the feeling of largeness or smallness as a shape is compared to its frame of reference.

On a page with many mini-compositions, we can have a shape that seems quite large in a moderately sized frame of reference (**A**). Without changing the frame of reference, we can reduce the physical size of the shape to gain more open space, reducing also its relative size (**B**), or increase the physical size of the shape so that it has to extend beyond the frame, making its relative size seem gigantic (**C**).

If we reduce the shape and the frame together, both the physical size of the shape and the frame diminish in scale simultaneously, but the shape's relative size is not affected. The now much physically smaller shape, inside the much smaller frame, still appears large in the crammed space (**D**).

If this small shape is transposed to a much larger frame, the smallness of the shape immediately becomes apparent (**E**). If there are even smaller shapes present inside the frame, the small shape becomes large again, being the largest shape in the composition (**F**).

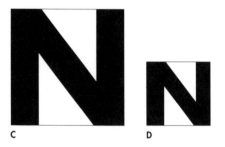

C   D

E

A

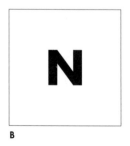

B

F

RELATIVE POSITION OF A SHAPE

As a shape is placed inside a frame of reference, it acquires a relative position, being seen as close to or far from one edge or one corner of the frame of reference.

It can be centrally located (**A**) or off-center (**B**). It can be close to the upper edge (**C**), the lower edge (**D**), the left edge (**E**), the right edge (**F**), the upper-left corner (**G**), the upper-right corner (**H**), the lower-left corner (**I**), or the lower-right corner (**J**), with different spatial effects.

A shape can move partially beyond an edge (**K**) or corner (**L**) of the frame of reference, so that a part is cropped off.

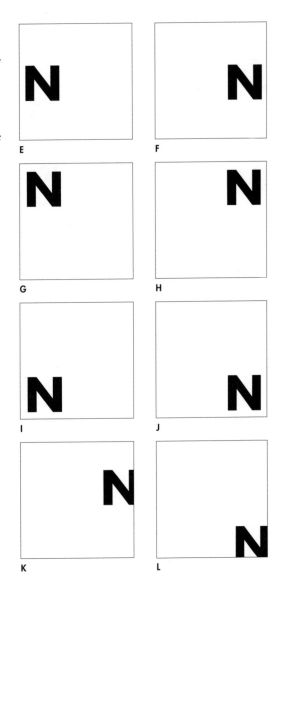

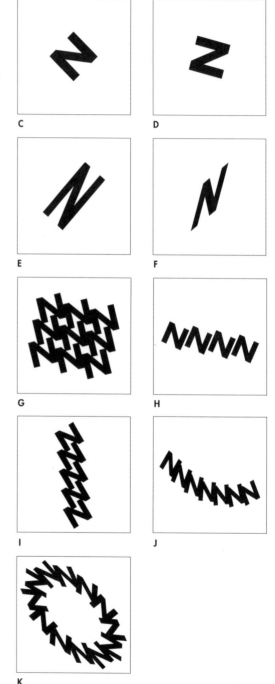

RELATIVE ORIENTATION OF A SHAPE

194

The rectangular or square frame of reference is generally seen with its left and right edges perpendicular to the ground on which we stand.

A shape may have an imaginary baseline, an imaginary axis, or a conspicuous edge for identification of its orientation. In general, its actual orientation is no different from its relative orientation, unless the frame of reference has no vertical or horizontal edges.

Orientation of a shape is often associated with our sense of stability and instability as affected by gravitational forces. If the shape's baseline is parallel to the horizontal edges of the frame of reference, it may appear stable (**A**, **B**). Tilting 45 degrees, it assumes a precarious balance (**C**). Tilting less or more than 45 degrees may suggest rising or falling movement (**D**).

A shape that is elongated or skewed can make a greater impact with its orientation (**E**, **F**). Units in any orientation can form a group, row, column, string, or ring that displays a separate orientation (**G** – **K**).

C

D

E

F

G

H

I

J

A

B

K

BACKGROUND

The entire area contained by the edges of the frame of reference is the background of the composition. It is continuous space stretching from top to bottom, left to right, and probably, with an illusion of depth, well behind the surface of the page.

As a shape appears inside the frame of reference, it covers a part of the background. The background may still show through if the shape has gaps or holes, and may be somewhat visible if the shape is not totally opaque.

On a page, if we use a shape tool to create a frame of reference, background is really the largest shape in the composition and looms behind all other shapes. It does not have to be white, but instead can be filled with a shade lighter (**A**), or darker (**B**), or very close to the shade of any other shape (**C**). It can also be in a pattern, although a pattern is more like a wall that may limit spatial recession (**D**).

A filled background may become positive space, with a white shape assuming a negative presence (**E**). The white shape, however, may turn positive when it has another shape behind it (**F**).

Background can be divided into two or more sections (**G**). A shape overlapping the divided background can be split at the junction of the sections (**H**).

There may not be any noticeable background when numerous shapes occupy the entire area (**I**).

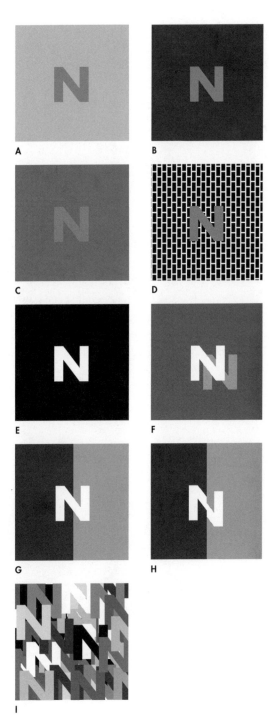

ASSIMILATION

196

Shapes in a composition can be related to one
another or to the background by way of *assimilation.* Assimilation occurs when we give adjacent
shapes, or shapes and their background, the same
fill or very similar fills so that they are seen linked
together, suggesting a bigger shape or one extended
area.

Very different shapes, such as the letter N and a
traced maple leaf, can be assimilated. We can fill
both in black and stroke them in white, interlocking them by slicing the N shape into two parts and
sending one part to the back of the leaf shape, and
then place them on an unfilled background. The
two shapes almost fuse with one another (**A**). If we
change the fill of the N shape to a medium gray,
each shape immediately becomes clearly distinguishable with no assimilation, but none of them is
yet assimilated with the background (**B**).

Filling the background in a shade similar to the N
shape restores assimilation, but now the N shape
appears to fuse more with the background than
with the leaf shape, which may not require a white
stroke to stand out (**C**).

A

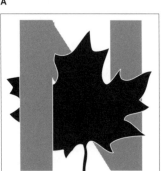

B

C

DISSIMILATION

The opposite of assimilation is *dissimilation*. When adjacent shapes, or shapes and the background, attain assimilation, what is not assimilated gets dissimilated. Dissimilation occurs when a shape differs considerably in shade or pattern from most other shapes and from the background, and may be increased with other visual contrasts.

Again using the N shape and the leaf shape, we can reduce the size of the leaf shape to show some dissimilation (**A**). The full effect of dissimilation is achieved when the N shape is assimilated with the background, with the leaf shape in a contrasting shade (**B**, **C**).

A

B

C

DOMINANCE

198

Assimilation and dissimilation are simple concepts that involve managing, primarily, shade, color, or tonal distribution in a composition. Assimilation may lead to some form of *dominance*, as assimilated shapes seem to fuse together and extend over a wide area, generally making the composition appear light, middle, or dark gray. The shapes may require additional emphasis to achieve full dominance.

Dominance is the clear assertion of unquestionable prominence. In most cases, it is achieved with largeness of size to generate an immediate impact. The dominant shape should not be assimilated with the background.

We can now use a large leaf shape along with a small N shape and give the leaf shape the dominant presence. The N shape may be seen as a detail of the leaf shape and somewhat lose its independence (**A**). We can make the leaf shape appear in multiple layers to enhance its visibility (**B**). When there are two leaf shapes, they cannot have equal prominence; one must dominate the other (**C**).

A

B

C

DISTINCTION

A dominant shape may be of secondary importance when another shape in the composition can catch more of the viewer's attention. A shape of *distinction* can be the smallest shape, but it must show strong dissimilation from all other shapes as well as from the background, and it must be in such a position as to be readily noticed, or so that all other shapes seem to lead to it.

Distinction puts a shape right in focus. The shape becomes the center of interest. It can still be forceful even if only shown in part (**A**). It is certainly more effective when no large shape dominates (**B**).

A dominant large shape can have a gradient fill so that one part with greater dissimilation establishes distinction in the composition (**C**).

A

B

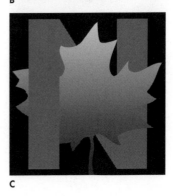

C

COMMUNICATION

200

Neither the N nor the leaf shapes in our demonstrations have been transformed or distorted to the extent that they are beyond recognition. They remain recognizable shapes and communicate at least on the most basic level: they are seen and recognized for what they are or what they represent.

On a higher level of communication, any shape in a composition must have a purpose and its visual characteristics should contribute to the fulfillment of that purpose.

Very often, words form a part of the composition. Communication thus becomes very direct, as words are meant to be read and instantly understood. They have sizes and attributes, however, and must be treated as shapes to work with other shapes, if any, and with the background. They may require distinction to be the main focal point in the design (**A** – **C**).

A

B

C

LEGIBILITY AND VISUAL EXPRESSION

Words may be the only shapes used in a composition. For communication, they should be generally legible so that the viewer can read them without much difficulty.

Maximum legibility requires the words to be of a considerable size, strongly dissimilated from the background, and occupying a central position. This may not always be desirable, as words are also shapes that need to be specially positioned, rotated, scaled, transformed, modified, stroked, and filled, to achieve a kind of visual expression that will appeal to targeted viewers.

Thus visual expression may take priority over legibility, which, however, should not be totally ignored. Our examples using the words "VISUAL DESIGN" in a composition show how the words are given maximum legibility (**A**), and how they are rotated, skewed, resized, repositioned, and variedly filled on a filled background to obtain a more interesting composition but with some compromise of legibility (**B**).

A

B

SPREADING SHAPES IN SPACE

202

Different compositions may be obtained by spreading shapes in space differently. Words as shapes of a comparatively small size can leave a wide-open background (**A**). They can, however, spread along the border of the frame of reference to further the feeling of spaciousness, in an *edge-conscious* composition (**B**).

We can overlap letters tightly in a band or bands to contrast them with unoccupied space in the composition (**C**). We can scale and stretch them to fill most of the space (**D – F**). We can also scatter them as individual shapes in an informal organization to cover most of the background (**G**).

B

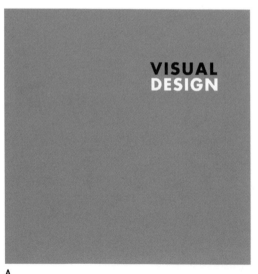

A

C

D

F

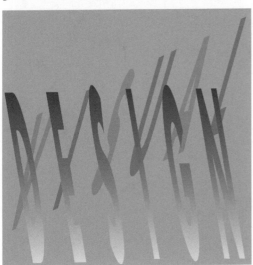

E

G

MULTIPLICATION

204

Multiplication refers to repeating the words in a composition. The words can appear in a structure that shows the order of repetition (**A**), gradation (**B**), radiation (**C**), or concentricity (**D**). Variation may be introduced, and we may have to give distinction to one group of words to assert a focal point.

Variation may be used to establish anomaly (**E**) or freely applied in an informal organization (**F**, **G**).

B

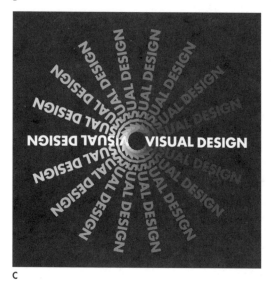

A

C

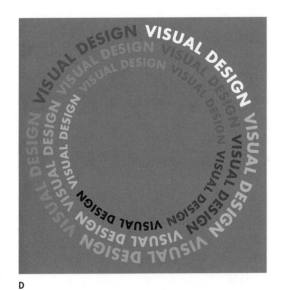

D

F

E

G

DIVISION

206

Division is a kind of disfiguration through arbitrary splitting of letters or words, frequently resulting in some reduction of their legibility (**A**).

We can split the background instead of splitting the letters or words. The words can overlap the divided background (**B**) or be rearranged and restrained by each section of the divided background (**C**).

We can divide the letters and the background into long strips or small planes and piece the strips or planes back together as in a collage. The clipping path can be used to clip different parts of the letter and the background in an irregular way (**D**), and the fragmented shapes can be contained in a frame (**E**).

Scale changes, reflections, and varied repetitions accompanying division can effect a strong sense of deconstruction, with the words intentionally and intriguingly ambiguous (**F**).

A

B

C

E

D

F

SYMBOLISM AND ASSOCIATION

208

Instead of using type exclusively, we can add shapes to strengthen communication. Shapes may have symbolic reference to particular persons, groups, institutions, companies, professions, events, activities, or human relationships. They may derive from forms found in our daily environment and can be associated with the meaning of the words in the composition.

For example, basic geometric figures, including the equilateral triangle, the circle, and the square, when used as a group, often symbolize visual design. We can bring these in to work with the words. They can form a column to replace the letter I in the word "DESIGN" (**A**). They can be repeated as rows or in layers in a formal organization (**B**, **C**). They can be less formally arranged (**D**), and may vary in size and attributes (**E**). We can adopt a deconstructivist approach, with a play of positive and negative shapes obliterating one another (**F**).

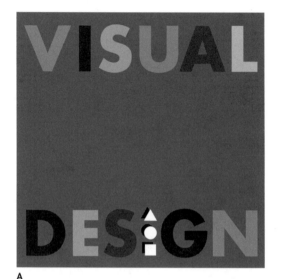

A

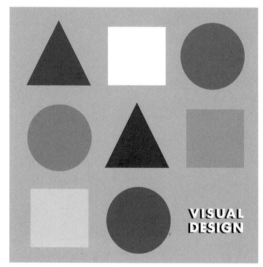

B

C

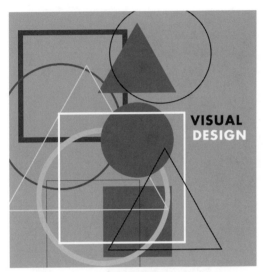

E

D

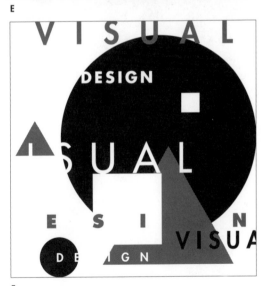

F

SUGGESTED PROBLEMS

210

Try using the word "DIRECTIONS," along with arrow shapes found in dingbat fonts or specially constructed if desired, to come up with a series of compositions that conform to the following requirements:

- Use the word without multiplication in a more central position (**A**).
- Spread the word with or without multiplication along the border of the frame of refence to attain an edge-conscious composition (**B**).
- Use the word with multiplication, employing a formal or semiformal organization, with varying degrees of assimilation with and dissimilation from the background (**C**, **D**).
- Make the arrow shapes dominate the composition (**E**, **F**).
- Use division in a deconstructivist approach (**G – I**).
- Feature one or more specially constructed arrow shapes to work with the word (**J**).

A

B

C

E

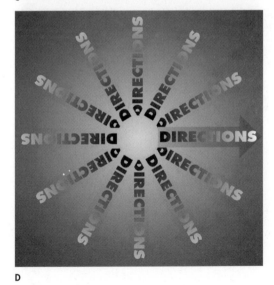

D

F

212

G

I

H

J

VISIBILITY AND ILLUSION

14

214   Visibility refers to how a shape is seen by the naked eye under normal lighting situations. Illusion refers to the suggestion of depth and volume in two-dimensional design. Both have to do with our perception and interpretation of space on a flat surface.

Shapes in a composition may have higher visibility or lower visibility, due to the degree of their dissimilation from the background and other shapes. Some shapes may appear to be closer or farther away than others if the background presents an illusion of depth.

Some shapes represent three-dimensional planes and volumes in a logical sequence with natural spatial illusions. In particular cases, such shapes may also be in an ambiguous arrangement or a situation that contradicts our daily visual experience.

For the purposes of communication and expression, we can manipulate the visibility and illusion of individual shapes or of the entire composition.

PERCEPTION OF SPACE

Visibility determines our perception of space. A shape of higher visibility appears closer to us than a shape of lower visibility, but much of the effect has to do with the shade of the background.

To demonstrate this, we can have a set of shapes, in 10-, 40-, 70-, and 100-percent black, and arrange them on backgrounds of 0 percent (unfilled), 50-percent, and 80-percent black. On unfilled and 20-percent black backgrounds, the 100-percent black shape is the most visible and also the closest (**A – B**). On a 50-percent black background, the 100-percent black shape is less visible than the 10-percent black shape (**C**). The same shape becomes, however, the least visible and the farthest away on an 80-percent black background (**D**).

We can now arrange the shapes with one slightly overlapping another. With the 100-percent black shape right in front, followed by those in 70-, 30-, and 10-percent black, spatial sequence appears natural on the unfilled and the 20-percent black background (**E**, **F**), but not quite natural on the 50-percent and 80-percent backgrounds (**G**, **H**).

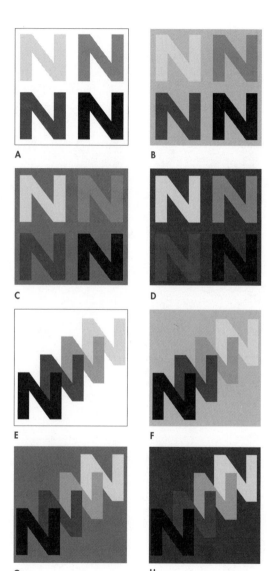

A

B

C

D

E

F

G

H

2 1 6

If we reverse the arrangement to have the 10-percent black shape in front and the l00-percent black shape at the back, then the spatial sequence on the unfilled, 20-percent and 50-percent black background may look somewhat unnatural (**I**, **J**), but may be perfectly natural on the 50-percent and 80-percent filled background (**K, L**).

Arranging the shapes in an order of 100-, 10-, 40-, and 70-percent may create an unnaturalness of spatial sequence on all backgrounds, except perhaps on the 50-percent background (**M – P**).

Unnatural spatial sequence is present on all backgrounds with the shapes arranged in the order of 40-, 70-, 10-, and 100-percent (**Q – T**).

A natural spatial sequence enhances the illusion of depth. A unnatural spatial sequence has ambiguous effects, which are sometimes preferable.

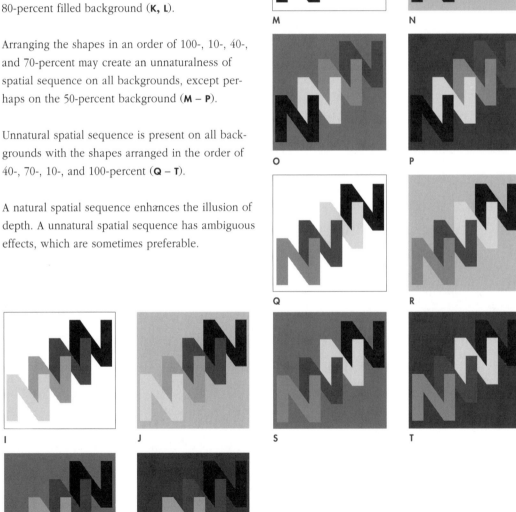

CONDITIONS OF VISIBILITY

Shapes in simple planes, and sharp-edge definitions with considerable dissimilation from one another and from the background, show good visibility (**A**). We can give high visibility to one chosen shape by assimilating all other shapes with the background (**B**).

The visibility of any shape may be reduced when the shape is partially overlapped by another shape (**C**), when it has blurred edges (**D**), or when the background is cluttered with too many shapes of similar sizes in an unnatural spatial sequence (**E**).

Visibility is considerably lowered when coarse textures or large patterns generally prevail (**G**), when there is a confusion of positive and negative space (**H**), and when most shapes show fragmentation (**I**).

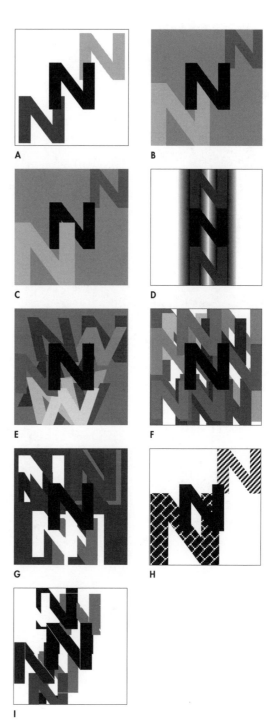

GRADIENT AND RADIAL FILLS

218

Gradient fills consist of smooth tonal changes in parallel transitions, from one chosen shade to another, in vertical, horizontal, or angled directions, effecting an illusion of changing lighting conditions and spatial curvature. A background with gradient fills, assimilating and dissimilating shapes in different areas, has variable effects on visibility (**A – C**).

The shapes can also have gradient fills, which usually reduce their general visibility. On a gradient-filled background, the shapes seem to curl, and turn up and down in space (**D – F**).

The background can be in two parts made with the rectangle tool. Each part has a separate gradient fill, and one part may be the reflection of the other, with the lightest or darkest area at their junction (**G – I**).

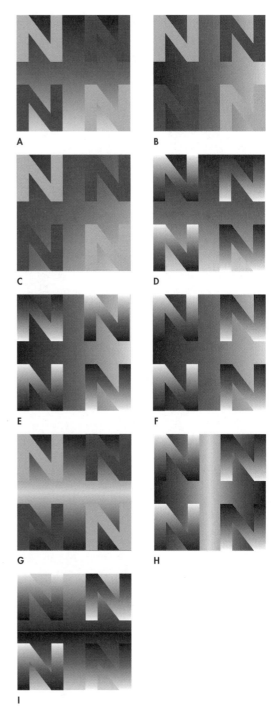

A

B

C

D

E

F

G

H

I

A background can be one flatly filled area extended with narrow gradient strips at two ends (**J**). It can consist of two flatly filled areas linked with a gradient strip in the middle (**K**), probably also with gradient strips at the two ends (**L**). Tonal progression of the gradients can be in opposite directions to form the background (**M**).

A radial fill, effecting the illusion of spherical concavity or convexity, consists of smooth tonal changes in concentric transitions, and may be regarded as a variation of the gradient fill. It can proceed from any shade to any other shade, without change in direction, and can be given to the background as well as the shapes (**N** – **O**). The starting shade usually lies at the center, but can be off-centered by using a clipping path (**P**). The background can be composed of two or more areas separately filled (**Q**).

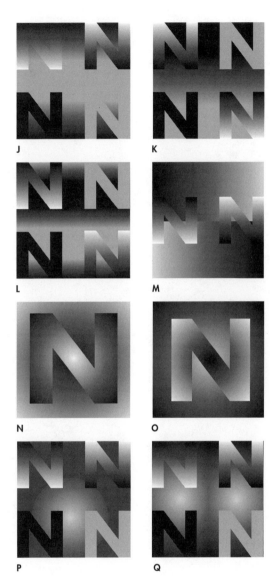

PATTERNED FILLS

220

Patterned fills are used when we wish to convey a more decorative feeling. Most drawing programs provide an assortment of stock patterns, which are miniature designs arranged in bit-mapped pixels that can be easily edited.

We can give patterned fills separately to individual shapes and to the background. Generally, patterns in black and white formed of lines and tiny planes in the background show little spatial recession, and tend to diminish visibility of the shapes if the shapes are also patterned.

Patterns composed of closely related lines or dots frequently stimulate our optic nerves with a scintillating effect, which may sometimes serve a specific design purpose (**A – D**).

Lines and dots of a pattern seen from a distance are perceived as one grainy shade. When adjacent patterns show grainy shades of similar density, they may not easily be distinguished from one another (**E – G**).

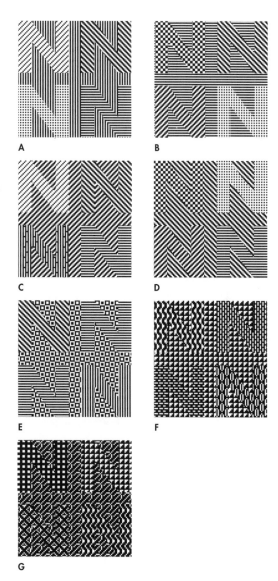

A

B

C

D

E

F

G

Bold patterns in the shape or the background can cause disintegration of the shapes (**H**, **I**). An extremely bold background pattern can overpower the foreground to the extent that the background may assume a more positive presence than the shapes (**J** – **L**).

Patterns in a draw program tend to remain unchanged no matter how the shape is rotated, reflected, scaled, or transformed. We can use a clipping path to fill different parts of a shape with different patterns (**M**), and can divide the background for a variety of patterned fills (**N**).

Some draw programs may allow using a *tile* command, the repetition of specially created shapes, in any desirable attributes, scale, and orientation, to form a patterned fill (**O**).

We can also use the line tool or any point tool to create a large area of linear patterns forming the general background, and use superimposed shapes as clipping paths. After clipping, the shapes can be shifted slightly in position to attain a bas-relief effect (**P**, **Q**).

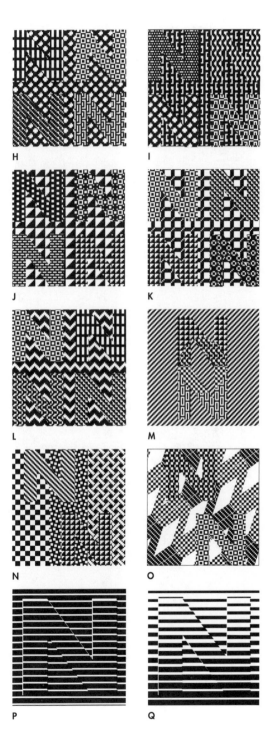

H

I

J

K

L

M

N

O

P

Q

MINIMUM VISIBILITY

222

Designs expressing an atmospheric or enigmatic feeling may have minimum visibility, which is attainable when all shapes tend to assimilate with one another and with the background, to the extent that they seem momentarily lost from sight.

We can achieve minimum visibility with very similar patterned fills (**A**). We can also use gradient fills (**B**), radial fills (**C**), or their combinations (**D**, **E**), with a resulting confinement to a narrow range of shades.

The background can be divided into separately filled sections for more complicated results (**F**, **G**).

B

A

C

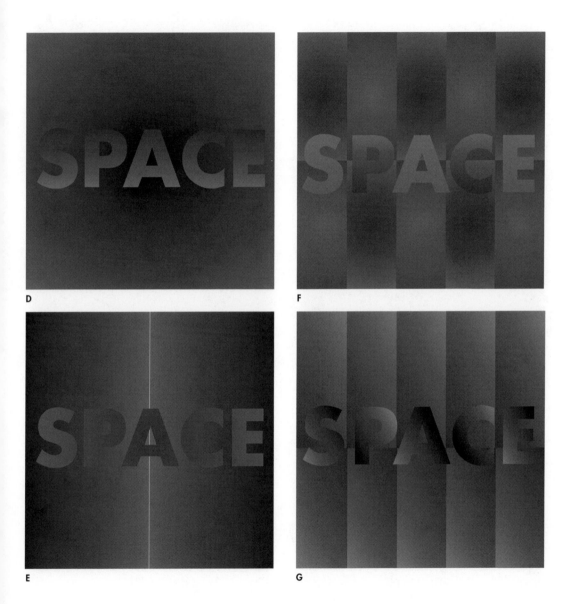

D

E

F

G

SPATIAL ILLUSIONS

2 2 4

Both gradient and radial fills lead to spatial illusions. The parallel tonal transitions of a gradient fill usually suggest cylindrical curvature (**A**, **B**), whereas the concentric tonal transitions of a radial fill show spherical curvature (**C**, **D**).

Such fills are instantly obtainable with the dialog box for attributes, but variations may be limited. We can, however, use the blend command to obtain similar effects, and achieve greater control with far wider possibilities.

As a demonstration, we can start with two identical thin lines to get a group of nine lines by using the blend command, and we can clone and reflect the group to obtain a total of eighteen lines (**E**). In each blend group, we can subselect either the starting or terminating line to assign attributes of line weight and shade. If the line weight is heavy enough, the blended result may be very similar to what is achieved with gradient fills (**F**). The lines can be lighter to allow the background to show through between the gaps (**G**). A gradient-filled background can be added behind the lines to create tonal transitions in a direction different from that of the blended lines (**H**).

We can blend a horizontal and a diagonal line to achieve a kind of spatial curvature that seems twisted (**I**). We can blend a rounded square with an elongated rounded rectangle, or a circle with an ellipse, resulting in concentric tonal transitions that may be more interesting than simple radial fills (**J**, **K**).

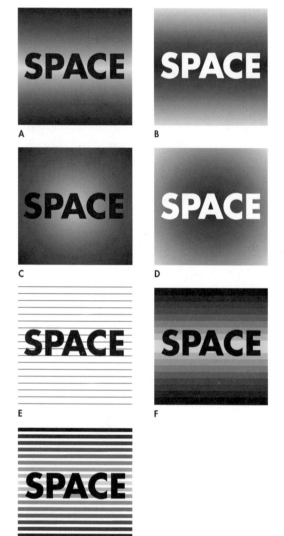

A

B

C

D

E

F

G

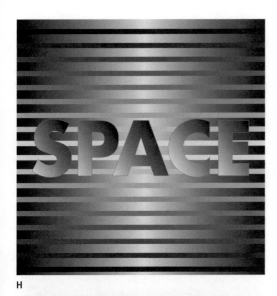

H

J

I

K

TRANSFORMATION OF SPACE

226

Blending is probably the easiest way to attain transformation of space. If we add a corner point to the starting line of a group of blended parallel lines, moving the point can immediately cause reblending of the entire group of lines, suggesting some kind of warped space (**A**).

The corner point can be replaced with a curve point if we want only smoothly flowing lines at that part of the composition, and we can add a corner point to the terminating line for effecting angular changes in a different location (**B**).

With changing attributes of the lines, with shifting points and handles associated with the lines, with moving, lengthening, or shortening the lines, and with inclusion of typographic elements to form compositions, there is virtually no limit to our exploration of possibilities (**C – J**).

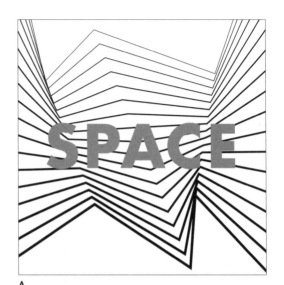

A

B

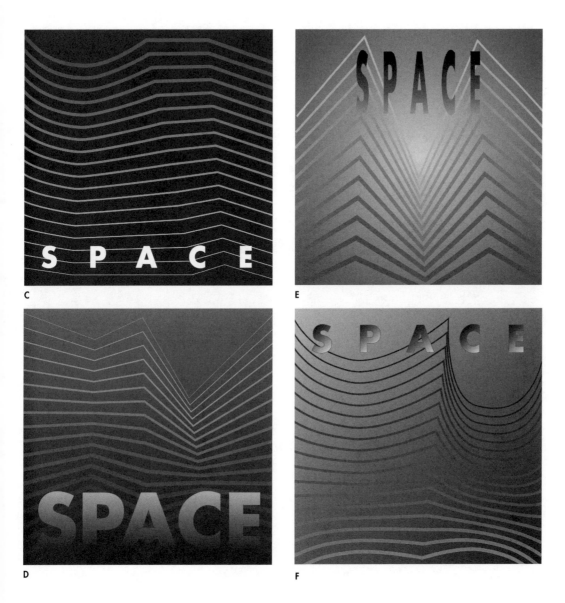

228

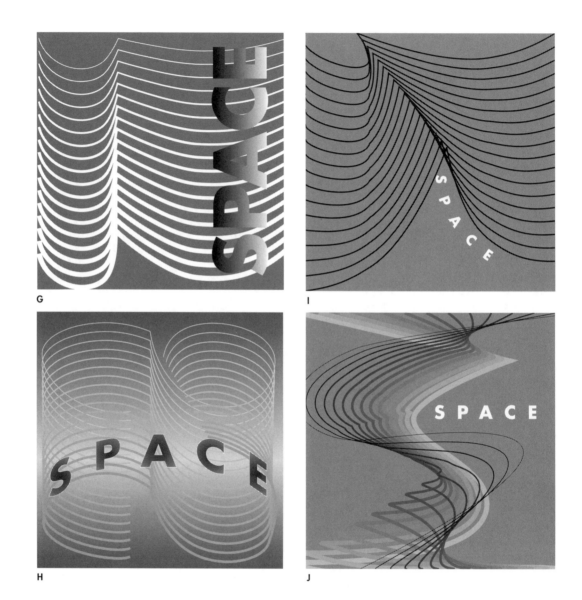

G

I

H

J

SPATIAL CONSTRUCTION WITH LINES

We can always extend a blend by cloning the terminating line and using it as a new starting line to blend with a new terminating line. The extended blend can have a similar or completely different configuration. A blend group or linked blend groups can be used as superunits in any kind of formal organization.

Blend groups can form a row, which is subsequently repeated to cover an area (**A**). Although the composition shows a repetition structure, the order of gradation is also evident, as there are always gradual changes in any blend. If we vary the shade of the starting or terminating line, the order of gradation may be further enhanced (**B**).

Repeated blend groups can show gradual change of size, width, or height in a gradation structure. For opaque overlapping, they can be backed with a shape or clipped with a closed path filled with white (**C**).

To establish a radiation structure, a blend group as a network of lines can be regularly rotated, with a lot of overlapping (**D**). If the blend group is in a wedge shape, or clipped by a clipping path in a wedge shape, it can be rotated in a full revolution, without overlapping (**E**).

A number of blend groups can form a ringlike enclosure. This can be repeated and enlarged or reduced in size and arranged in the order of concentricity (**F**).

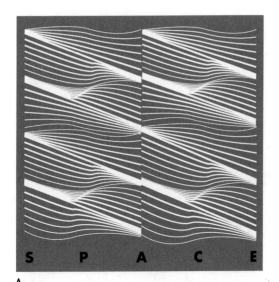

A

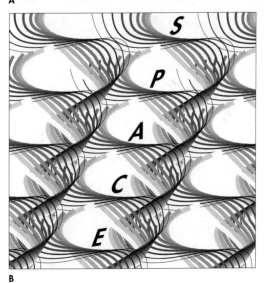

B

230

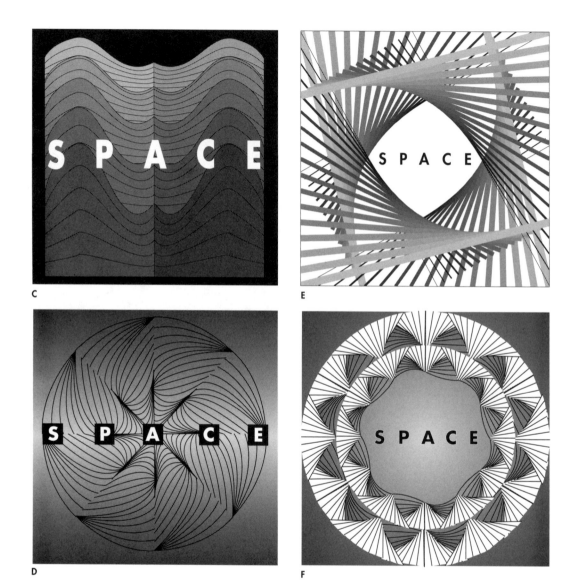

C

E

D

F

SPATIAL CONSTRUCTION WITH PLANES

Squares and rectangles made with the rectangle tool can be skewed 45 degrees vertically or horizontally, to become a parallelogram for use as a set of basic planes for spatial construction.

Four unfilled parallelograms in different orientations can form a transparent cube. Four of these transparent cubes, stacked, may be seen as a bigger cube with internal planes subdividing the volume (**A**).

The outlined parallelograms can be filled and used as opaque planes. We can arrange them in an orderly way to create the illusion of a cube or a group of cubes related to our normal vision, with reference to a definite light source (**B, C**). If the planes are just freely filled with shades, the light source becomes uncertain, but the cubes are still naturally presented (**D**).

If the planes remain unfilled, they form a linear framework that does not isolate or contain space. Changing the shade of the strokes for one of the stacked cubes may create spatial ambiguity. Such ambiguity can be made more interesting with type casting a long shadow behind to suggest spatial depth in the composition (**E**).

One or more filled planes in the group of stacked cubes can be brought to the front, so that a plane forming the bottom of one cube also forms the top of another cube, resulting in a jarring vision (**F, G**). The presentation of space is illogical, but can have unusual visual dynamics.

We can have adjacent cubes in totally different orientations so that the natural vision is twisted (**H**). Internal planes inside the illogically arranged cubes can further the effect of conflicting spatial illusions (**I**). Filling the background with a bold pattern can push the shapes towards the viewer.

A

232

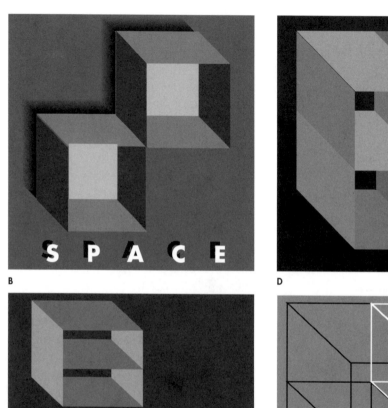

B

D

C

E

F

H

G

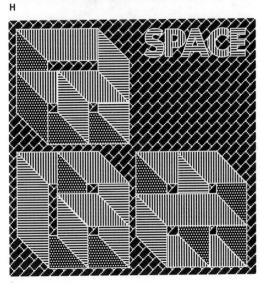

I

SKEWING TYPE FOR ILLUSORY EFFECTS

234

We can skew type in the same way as we skew a plane. Four lines of letters, differently skewed and in different shades, can easily form a hollowed, elongated cube or a prismatic tube (**A**).

The skewed letters can be rotated to attain the order of radiation. The illusion of depth may be enhanced with type in a gradient fill (**B**).

Each letter can be separately skewed. The result may suggest individual letters in a line bending alternately inward or outward in space (**C**).

Each line of letters can be accompanied with a shadow obtained with disproportionate scaling and skewing. The shadows can be given unusual prominence for a unique illusory effect (**D**).

Three lines of letters can be skewed as oblique planes to form a triangle. They conflict with one another spatially, especially when we duplicate them and have them interlocked (**E**).

A natural-looking cube can be constructed with three lines of letters in a condensed style skewed 60 degrees and progressively rotated 120 degrees (**F**). If gaps between the letters are not significant, an illusion of volume can be established.

A

B

C

D

E

F

BUILDING VOLUME WITH TYPE

236

The illusion of volume may be created more easily with type repeated in multiple layers. This is exactly the way zoom text is effected (see the section in chapter 6 on Special Effects, page 80). Without using zoom text, we can fill layers with a gradual shade change, or even use gradient fills to establish light and shade (**A**).

We can show volume in an oblique view by skewing the letters before adding the layers. The layers can appear in any direction. The entire line of letters can appear to tilt toward the viewer (**B**) or to shift away from the picture plane (**C**).

If the layers of letters are only stroked but not filled, the outlines can form a transparent volume. If a fluctuating spatial illusion is desirable, the outlines of individual letters can be a gradation of line weights, in alternating directions (**D**). Opaque layers can also be arranged so that the volumes formed by the line of letters show alternating views (**E**, **F**).

Layers can be made gradually smaller to suggest the illusion of one-point perspective. This can be accomplished with power duplication, after initial cloning, scaling, and shifting of position (**G**). We can have skewed letters with expanding layers for less naturalistic effects (**H**).

Negative volume is suggested if layers are behind an opaque plane containing the letters as holes or openings (**I**). The holes or openings can be obtained by joining the letters and planes together after ungrouping them.

Layers can vary in size, proportion, position, or direction, to form volumes that are not shaped with straight edges (**J**).

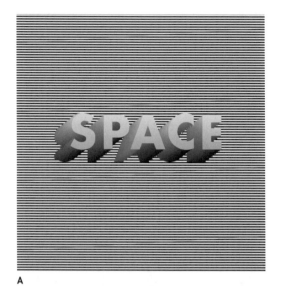

A

B

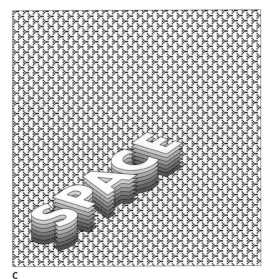

C

D

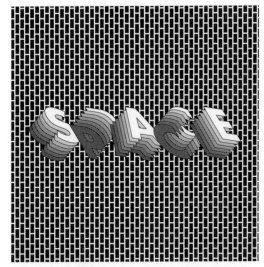

E

F

238

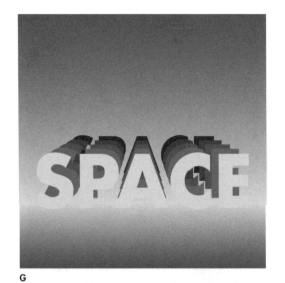

G

I

H

J

DISTORTING TYPE

Type can be joined to a curved path and skewed vertically, resulting in cylindrical distortion. Layers can then be added to obtain a curved volume (**A**).

If type is joined to a circle or ellipse, a hollowed cylinder can be accomplished. The illusion can be enhanced if the letters show gradual shade change (**B**).

A curved line of letters can be extended with repetition. Gradient fills can be applied to the letters so that each letter also appears individually curled. (**C**).

An illusion of a curved wall in perspective requires each letter to be scaled progressively taller, with subsequent manual manipulation of the points or paths (**D**).

Distorted letters in layers forming a group can be cloned and rotated 180 degrees to achieve an illusion of twisted space (**E**).

The layers of letters can be shifted to form a distorted volume (**F**)

A

B

240

C

E

D

F

SUGGESTED PROBLEMS

Try using the word "STEPS" as a shape to develop a series of compositions that conform to the following requirements:

- Use the word in layers to form an illusion of steps (**A**).
- Use the word in a series of planes with skewing transformations to construct the steps (**B**).
- Distort the word through repetition and, if desired, further transformation to create the illusion of curved steps (**C**).
- Use the rectangle tool to construct solidly filled planes forming the step pattern, featuring low visibility (**D**).
- Use the rectangle tool to construct a linear framework in the step pattern, showing some degree of spatial ambiguity or conflicting visual effects (**E**).
- Blend lines as planes to create the step illusion (**F**).

A

B

242

C

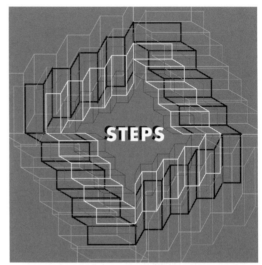

E

D

F

15

2 4 4

Design rarely ends with the image displayed on the computer screen, which is no more than an electronic rendering of our efforts. This image will not acquire any tangible form until it becomes a hard copy on paper. Printing the design is part of the design process, and this can be done conveniently with a laser printer directly connected to the computer.

Although the electronic rendering is referred to as WYSIWYG (what you see is what you get), discrepancies between the screen image and the printed image do exist. Such discrepancies are noticeable in tonal contrasts, line weights, and edge definitions of shapes, and sometimes also in positioning and alignment of elements, and configurations of fonts.

As the design gets printed, all probable discrepancies must be checked and general details examined. Any rectification and revision will require further printing to revalidate the results. Final printing may be done on special paper if necessary.

Post-printing treatment may include trimming and folding of the paper, along with any additional work needed to prepare the design for final presentation.

LASER PRINTING

A laser printer uses a laser beam to form an image on a photosensitive metal drum. The image is then made visible by electrostatically attracting dry ink-powder to it. The process is very similar to that used in a photocopier.

Most laser printers can interpret the PostScript language, have a range of resident fonts, and provide a reasonably high resolution, commonly 300 dpi, which is more than four times the resolution of the screen display. Some printers can give a resolution as high as 600 dpi, a quality that approaches commercial printing.

CHOICE OF PAPER

Paper in letter size (8^1/$_2$- x 11 inches) is the most common for laser printing. There are larger printers that can handle the tabloid size (11- x 17 inches). Most kinds of paper with a smooth surface can be laser printed, but the weight of paper must range from 16 to 41 pounds, equivalent to 60 to 157 grams per square meter (g/m^2), to avoid jamming.

For crisp output, you can use paper specially made for laser printing. To achieve unique results in final printing, you might also consider paper of different colors, surface textures, and weights, including translucent tracing paper and transparent film. In a multiple-page design, special effects can be attained with a mixture of plain and colored paper (**A**), translucent tracing paper (**B**), or transparent film (**C**).

A

B

C

HALFTONE SCREENS

246

All strokes and fills with gray shades and grayscale photographic images are usually printed with a halftone screen pattern to simulate the gray levels.

The halftone screen has a resolution standard different from the resolution of the printer and the bit-mapped computer screen. It is composed of matrixed lines of tiny dots usually seen as round. The number of such matrixed lines per running inch, referred to as *lpi*, make up the *screen ruling*, or the *screen frequency*, which determines the screen resolution. A laser printer with a 300-dpi resolution can at best print a halftone screen of 60-lpi resolution, as each halftone dot requires a number of laser dots to build the shape. In commercial printing, the halftone screen can be as fine as 133 lpi and above.

Apart from the screen ruling, there is also the *screen angle*, normally at 45 degrees. Variation of screen angle is possible, and actually necessary for multiple color overlays in commercial printing to avoid creation of unwanted moiré patterns.

Furthermore, there are different screen types. The default dot screen has a pattern of both black and white round dots (**A**). We can, however, have the line screen composed of parallel straight lines (**B**). Screens composed of elliptical, square, triangular, and other dot patterns are less common but may also be available.

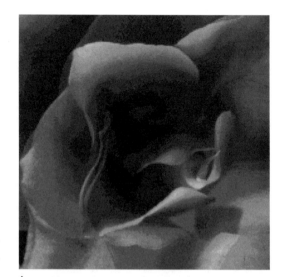

A

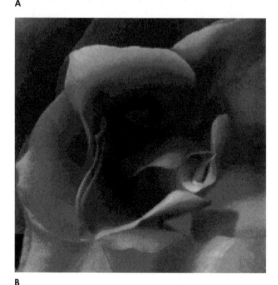

B

DITHERING THE IMAGE

Any scanned photographic image that has been properly adjusted in tonal contrast (**A**) or arbitrarily modified (**B**) can be dithered to obtain special graphic effects (see the section in chapter 8 on photographic images, page 108). We may be able to dither the image with halftone dot and line patterns in a draw program, choosing different screen angles and coarse screen rulings, and preview the results (**C – J**).

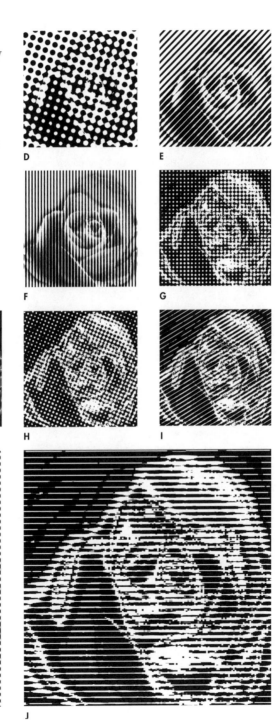

A

B

C

D

E

F

G

H

I

J

248

The dithered image obtained in a draw program can be in any shade and resized or disproportionately rescaled without affecting the screen angle or screen ruling of the halftone pattern (**K**). The background of the image is usually opaque. To make its background transparent, we may have to transfer the image to a paint program, and subsequently cut it and paste it back to the draw program for superimposition on any filled shape or area (**L**, **M**). The image is now bit-mapped, and its halftone pattern can be distorted with rescaling (**N**).

In an image-editing program, we may be able to dither the photographic image or any grayscale image directly with bit-mapped dot patterns in a desired resolution (**O**, **P**). The resultant image usually has a transparent background. It can be resized or rescaled, but the pattern structure is invariably affected (**Q**).

We can use the original photographic image in a design (**R**), but we can also use dithered images that are previewable. Our examples show compositions incorporating a dithered image in error diffusion with a radial fill (**S**), in 45-degree line (**T**), in 45-degree line with radial fill (**U**), in Bayer with patterned fill (**V**), in 0-degree default dot with sectioned tonal fills (**W**), in 45-degree default dot with prior arbitrary tonal manipulation (**X**), and in 0-degree default dot with double reflections and a radial fill (**Y**).

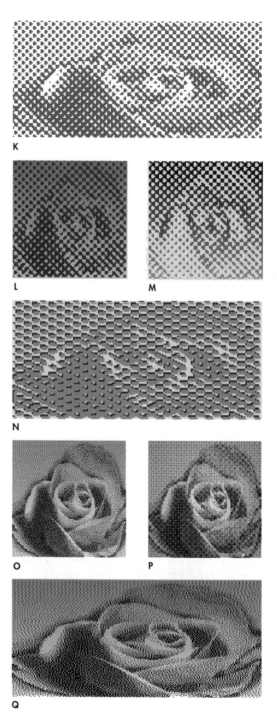

K

L

M

N

O

P

Q

R

T

S

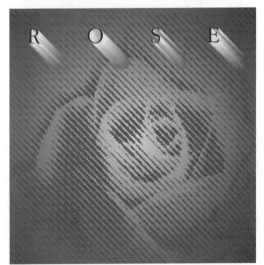

U

250

V

X

W

Y

POST-PRINTING TREATMENT

Post-printing treatment prepares the printed design for presentation and adds a finishing touch.

Although we can print designs on two sides of the same piece of paper with the laser printer, accurate alignment is rarely achieved, and we may have to paste two sheets of printed images back to back.

Paper needs trimming to a specific size, and may get folded. If the design is of considerable size or consists of multiple pages, we may have to glue the edges or two or more sheets of paper together. A booklet usually requires stapling or stitching. A design may be in the form of a tube or container, or may have shaped edges, holes, or slits.

FOLDING

Folding divides a surface into clearly definable areas, each having its separate frame of reference, and the design thus acquires a three-dimensional articulation.

A design with both sides printed contains four pages with one simple fold. A composition can occupy one page, but can also spread to two adjacent pages. Individual compositions on each page must all be visually related to attain unity.

Paper may have a vertical (**A**), horizontal (**B**), or diagonal fold (**C**). In the latter case, a square sheet becomes triangular.

Paper may also have two or more folds (**D** – **G**). Thin paper can be folded in layers to achieve unusual configurations (**H** – **L**).

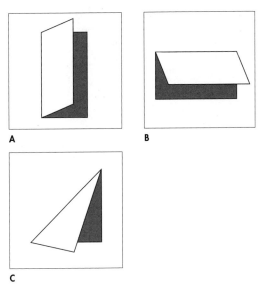

A

B

C

252

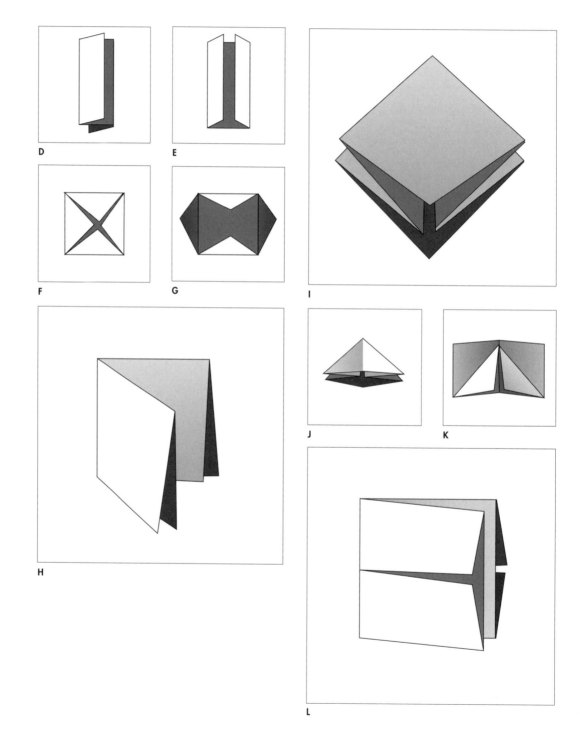

D

E

F

G

I

H

J

K

L

ANGLED TRIMS

Paper is normally trimmed at right angles, but can also be trimmed at an angle with all edges remaining straight. Angled trims can be applied to one edge (**A** – **C**), one corner (**D** – **F**), two edges (**G** – **I**), or two corners (**J** – **L**), resulting in different shapes with different folded effects.

An angled trim makes possible the partial showing of any underlying inner page after the paper is folded, and this can affect the compositions of individual pages.

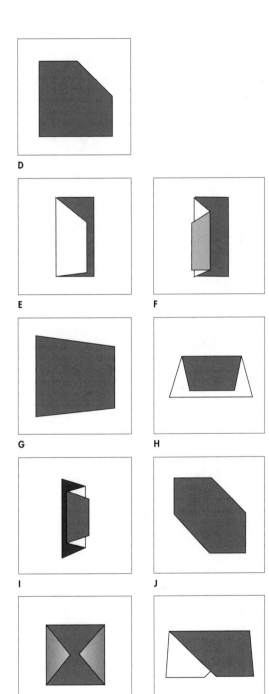

D

E

F

G

H

A

B

C

I

J

K

L

DIE-CUTS

254   We can make holes on the surface of paper (**A**, **B**), shape the edges of the paper (**C**, **D**), or introduce both holes and shaped edges (**E**, **F**). The paper can be cut in a special shape after it is folded (**G**, **H**).

The holes and shaped edges are generally referred to as *die-cuts*, the term used in commercial printing, although we make the cuts manually with a knife or a pair of scissors.

As in cases with angled trims, inner pages may show through after folding. When there is more than one hole, the larger hole can reveal the smaller hole, which may further reveal an underlying inner page (**I – J**).

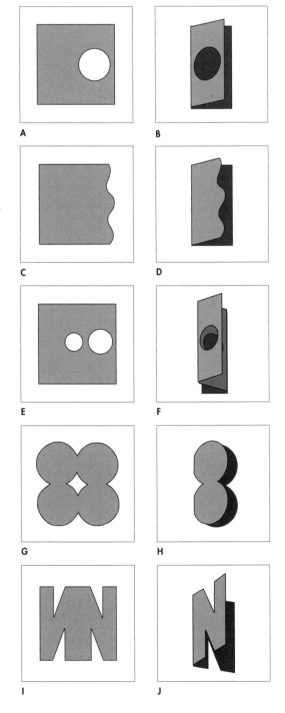

A

B

C

D

E

F

G

H

I

J

SLITS

The making of a slit on the surface or along an edge of the sheet of paper is also part of the die-cutting process.

The slit can occur at the edge (**A**, **B**) or on the surface of the paper (**C**, **D**) to facilitate special folds.

Folding with a slit opening can create a three-dimensional effect with creasing and bending (**E** – **H**).

Two opposite edges of the sheet of paper can be interlocked with slits (**I**, **J**). Slits can be in a circular or any specially designed shape (**K** – **N**).

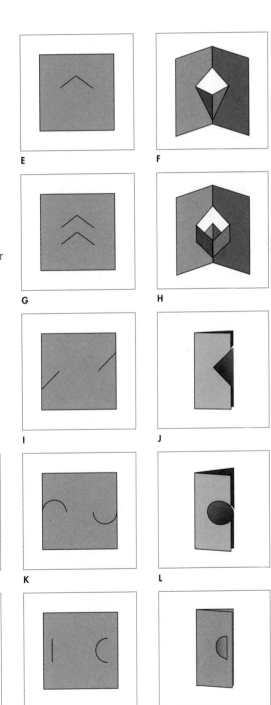

E

F

G

H

I

J

A

B

K

L

C

D

M

N

MULTIPLE PAGES

256

A multiple-page design in a presentation may require that sheets of paper be joined to make an accordion fold (**A**, **B**) or other kinds of folds (**C** – **F**). It may consist of separate sheets loosely nested (**G**, **H**) or securely bound together.

Compositions on multiple pages should have stylistic consistency, so that designs on different pages are completely related and can be seen as a whole. They can express a common theme with variations (**I**), with pictorial continuity (**J**), or in a sequence of space/time events (**K**).

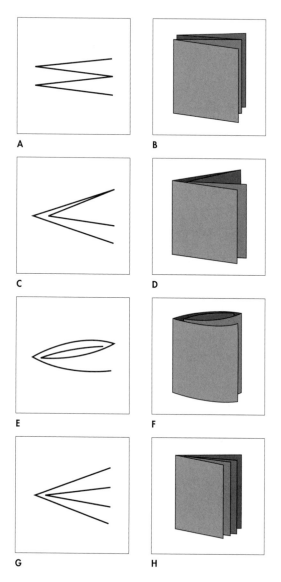

A

B

C

D

E

F

G

H

I

J

K

SUGGESTED PROBLEMS

Try developing a multiple-page design. The design should be in an accordion fold, printed on one or both sides, with or without die-cut shapes, expressing one of the following themes:

- Water – shapes and patterns that suggest water, such as drops, condensation, ripples, waves, or swirls (**A**).
- Keys – an arrangement of scanned images of photo-copied keys, with dithering manipulations (**B**).
- Shadows – representational or abstract shapes associated with shadows, which give illusory depth to the background space (**C**).
- From A to Z – using type of one or more fonts in a sequence of compositions with one letter leading to the next, showing the similarities, contrasts, and probable variations (**D**).

Instead of choosing from the themes just described, develop a theme by referring to one of the following broad categories:

- Nature, including any natural phenomena; flowers, trees, plants, animals, birds, insects, reptiles, fish, sea shells, mountains, rivers, landscapes, and the universe.
- Objects, including anything that can be found around us; furniture, tools, machine parts, stationery, books, cars, boats, and so forth.
- Man-made environments, ranging from the city, highways, roads, buildings, and houses, to windows, doors, or entrances.
- Parts of the body, including hands, feet, faces, and so on.
- Human relations, including expressions of love, hatred, anger, joy, sadness, solitude, friendship, and other feelings.
- Time, such as hours of the day, months or seasons of the year, decades, centuries, or eras, as related to personal or general experiences.
- Culture, including subjects related to the arts, religion, social customs, and the history of mankind.
- Perception and fantasy, referring to what is actually seen and what is just an illusion; scenes from the imagination, dreams, and hallucinations.
- Writing, including all forms of written expressions; words, individual characters, calligraphy, and pictographs.
- Shapes, including all geometric figures, freely formed flat shapes, and three-dimensional forms and structures.

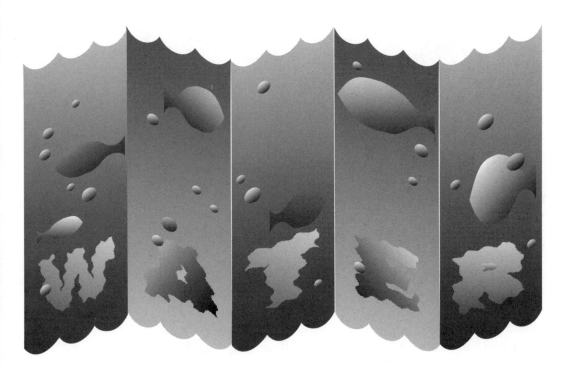

A

B

260

C

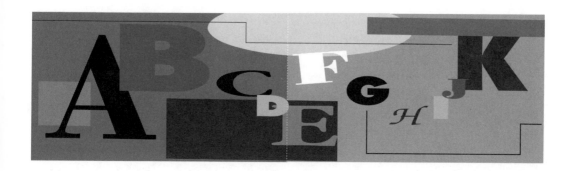

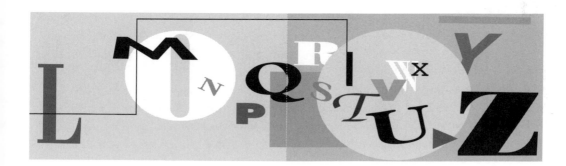

D

PURSUING FURTHER DEVELOPMENT

262

The problems suggested in this chapter and various preceding chapters aim at providing no more than a modest start in design. To pursue further development as a designer, the reader must look into the functional aspects of design, which can encompass one or more of the following:

- Conveying information
- Communicating a persuasive message
- Selling a product or a service
- Targeting a specific sector of the community
- Efficient fulfillment of a particular purpose
- Economic means of production

Designs may be created in such categories as posters, advertisements, book covers, logos, or brochures and have definite practical applications. They are probably judged more on how they meet business requirements or fulfill commercial aims than on their aesthetic merits.

Working with the computer, the need for a wider range of software programs will definitely grow with time. Programs that are in current use may require periodic upgrading to take advantage of new and extended features.

With increased experience and proficiency, any computer user may, sooner or later, have to look into acquiring more peripherals and installing additional memory chips and accelerators in the central processing unit to gain convenience and to improve speed and performance. In time, we shall all have to consider replacement of our entire computer system as major technological breakthroughs occur.

Finally, however, one thing must be made clear: good design can be created with or without the help of the computer. The computer, after all, is only a tool. It is the means, but not the end. Although the computer may help realization of the idea and facilitates quick visualization of alternative compositions, what is far more important is the idea that determines the design, and the designer's aesthetic sensibility that guides the composition.

Aggregate. A group of two or more shapes brought together to be seen as one visual entity.

Anomaly. Irregularity in a design where regularity generally prevails.

Ascender. Portion of a lowercase letter extending above the general height.

Assimilation. Close tonal relationship of a shape with the background or any adjacent shape.

Attribute. Visual appearance of a line or shape that can be assigned with computer commands.

Axis. An imaginary straight line that crosses the middle of a shape, dividing it into two halves, each being the mirror image of the other; or an imaginary straight line along which a shape is reflected.

Background. Space behind lines or shapes in a composition, contained within a frame of reference.

Baseline. Invisible line on which all letters stand.

Bit-mapped image. Image displayed on the computer screen, composed of tiny square dots.

Blend. Group of lines or shapes showing gradual changes, obtained with a command.

Cap. Shape present at or added to an end of a line.

Character. Letter, number, or symbol, obtainable with the keyboard; or any basic component of our written language.

Clipping path. A closed path used to crop any line, shape, or image it overlaps.

Clone. An exact copy of a line or shape.

Closed path. A path that makes a complete enclosure, containing no end points.

Component. Line or shape serving as part of an aggregate or superunit.

Composite shape. A group of shapes joined together, taking on the same attributes and frequently showing holes where the shapes overlap.

Composition. The total visual effect of lines and shapes in specific attributes, locations, orientations, interacting with one another on a background.

Concentricity structure. A structure with layers of shapes that increase or decrease progressively in size, or with rings of shapes as expanding or contracting layers.

Configuration. General appearance of a shape described by its contours.

Connector point. A kind of point at the join of a straight path and a curved path, providing smooth linkage.

Contrast. Any difference that helps us to distinguish elements, lines, or shapes.

Control handle. A floating handle associated with a point, used to adjust the curvilinearity of a path.

Corner point. A kind of point acting as a hinge at the join of two paths.

Curve point. A kind of point effecting a smooth flow, removing angularity at the join of two paths.

Deconstruction. Breaking up a structure with partial or total demolition of its spatial order.

Descender. Portion of a lowercase letter extending below the baseline.

Die-cut. Slits, holes, or special shapes made on the surface or edge of paper during the printing process.

Dilation. Increasing the size of a shape.

Direction. Orientation measurable in angle of degrees.

Disfiguration. Deforming or disintegrating a shape.

Dissimilation. Contrasting tonal relationship of a shape with the background or any adjacent shape.

Distinction. Conspicuous presence of a line or shape, usually marking the focal point in a position.

Dithering. Conversion of a grayscale image into a bit-mapped image composed of dot or line patterns.

Division. Splitting a shape into two or more separable parts.

Dominance. Overwhelming presence of a shape or a group of shapes occupying the biggest area of space in a composition.

Dot. A tiny, visible shape, usually in a simple configuration.

Dpi. Dots per inch, a unit measurement for screen display and printing resolutions.

Edge. Border of a line or shape.

Element. Point or path constituting a line or shape.

End. The starting or terminating part of a line.

File format. A standardized way of storing visual documents in the computer for future use or for further manipulation.

Fill. Color, shade, gradient, pattern, or texture that occupies the space enclosed by a closed path; one of the attributes of a shape.

Font. A collection of type in a specially designed style.

Form. Any visual entity that seems to assume independent physical existence in space.

Formal organization. Arrangement of lines or shapes with strict regularity.

Frame of reference. Border defining the area and shape of a composition.

Gradation. Gradual sequential change in one or more visual or spatial aspects.

Gradation structure. Structure that constrains the arrangement of lines or shapes in gradually increasing or decreasing horizontal and/or vertical distances from one another.

Gradient. A fill showing gradual tonal or color changes.

Grayscale. Range of gray shades as percentages of black.

Grid. Non-printing lines or dots in a regular pattern to help arrange shapes in a formal organization.

Halftone. Dot or line pattern used in printing to represent grayscale, particularly in the reproduction of photographs.

Illusion. Depth, volume, or spatial curvature that seems to exist on the flat surface of the paper containing the design.

Image. Any visible entity, whether clearly seen or barely discernible.

Informal organization. Arrangement of lines or shapes without a structure.

Join. Junction of two lines showing a protrusion.

Layer. Sequential arrangement of shapes, with one above or behind another, showing illusory depth.

Legibility. Clarity; ability of type to communicate without difficulty.

Letter. Individual character that forms part of a word.

Line. A path that becomes visible after stroking with weight as well as color, shade, or pattern.

Location. Position of an element, line, or shape inside the frame of reference.

Lpi. Lines per inch, a unit of measurement for screen ruling or frequency in halftones.

Multiplication. Repeated use of a line or shape.

Negative shape. A shape that appears as a hole or gap with the background showing through.

Object. Line or shape that can be selected individually in a draw program.

Open path. A path that does not enclose space and that has two unconnected end points.

Orientation. General direction of a line or shape.

Outline. A closed path that becomes visible after stroking with weight as well as color, shade, or texture, representing the contour of a shape.

Path. Straight or curved linear linkage between any two adjacent points. This becomes a visible line upon stroking with weight and color, shade, or pattern.

Pattern. Regularly repeated dots or lines that can cover a line or shape as part of its attributes.

Picture plane. An imaginary plane defined by a frame of reference, coinciding with the physical surface of the paper or screen displaying the lines or shapes.

Pixel. Picture element forming the screen display. There are 72 pixels to a linear inch.

Plane. Surface filled with a color, shade, gradient, pattern, or texture, enclosed by a closed path.

Point. An anchoring element used to determine the position of different parts of a path, with a constraining effect to its shape. It is also a unit (72 points to an inch), used in measuring type sizes and line weight.

Position. General location of a line or shape.

Positive shape. A shape that occupies space, usually blocking any other shape lying behind.

PostScript. A computer language developed by Adobe Systems, sent to printers to produce high-resolution output.

Power duplication. Progressive repetition of an operation by the computer, combining position and possibly other changes.

Radiation structure. Structure that constrains the arrangement of rotating lines or shapes with reference to a common center.

Reflection. Flipping to change a shape to its mirror image.

Repetition structure. Structure that constrains the arrangement of lines or shapes in equal horizontal distances as well as vertical distances from one another.

Resolution. Degree of fineness or coarseness in screen display or in printing of computer-generated lines, shapes, or images.

Rotation. Change in orientation of a line or shape.

Scale. Size and proportion of a shape.

Semiformal organization. Arrangement of shapes using a structure along with the introduction of free variations or irregularity.

Serial dilation. Repetition of a shape in a regular, concentric sequence, with gradual change of its size.

Serial gradation. Repetition of a line or shape in a regular sequence, with gradual changes in one or more of its visual or spatial aspects.

Serial reflection. Reflection of a line or shape in a regular sequence along alternate axes of different orientations.

Serial rotation. Progressive rotation of a line or shape in a regular sequence to form a partial or full revolution around a common center.

Serial translation. Repetition of a line or shape in a regular sequence and forming a row or column.

Shape. Any distinguishable visual entity composed of paths.

Similarity. Presence of resemblance in one or more visual aspects.

Size. Dimensions of a shape.

Spatial aspects. Spatial situations of a line or shape, including its position, orientation, layering order, and apparent progression or recession in illusory space.

Stroke. Independent line or outline of a shape assigned weight as well as color, shade, pattern, or texture.

Structure. Order of arrangement that produces strict spatial regularity.

Subdivision. An area of space defined with structural lines.

Superunit. A composite or aggregate used repeatedly.

Symmetry. Formal relationship of elements in mathematical order of translation, reflection, rotation, or dilation.

Texture. Dots, lines, or tiny shapes spreading evenly or unevenly over a surface.

Theme. Subject or topic communicated or expressed in a design.

Translation. Change of position of a line or shape.

Type. Any character originated with the keyboard.

Unit. Line or shape used repeatedly.

Visibility. Distinguishable appearance of an image or shape.

Visual aspects. Visual characteristics of a line or shape, including its general configuration, size, and attributes.

Visual order. A state of regularity achieved by relating shapes both visually and spatially.

Visual relationship. Relationship of shapes in their visual aspects, as repetition, gradation, or similarity.

Weight. Thickness of a line.

X-height. Height of type measured from the baseline to the top of lowercase letters, excluding ascenders and descenders.